College Survivor

*"Learning the Art and Strategy of Earning
Scholarships and Grants from Kindergarten
to Grad School and Beyond."*
P. Solis-Friederich

"Give a man a fish,
and you feed him for
a day. Teach a man
to fish, and you feed
him for a lifetime."

– Chinese Proverb

© Strategies for Excellence, LLC dba College Survivor

Print ISBN: 978-1-54393-789-3

eBook ISBN: 978-1-54393-790-9

Dedicated to

My #1 Fan

Dad

ACKNOWLEDGEMENTS

My Savior, Jesus Christ. You created me!

My Family, husband, children, parents, siblings, and in-laws. You are my rocks!

My Wakeup, the birth of our youngest son. You gave me strength!

My Support, Ruben and Bernadette Solis. You believed in me!

My Heart, Margot Peña-Zuniga . You taught me how to be "smart poor"!

My Mentor, Pat McGill. You reignited my fire!

My Advocate, Judith Stanton. You pulled me out of the dark!

My Corporate Mentor, Felix Salazar. You molded me!

My College Professor, Glynis Holm Strause. You showed me the path!

My Childhood Core, Refugio High School. You taught me how to be a champion!

TESTIMONIES

*"I've long believed that a college education is more valuable and attainable than many people might think. **Phyllis takes the Why and the What of making a college education affordable, and brings the HOW to life in this amazingly detailed guide.** The strategies and implementation tactics in this resource will be a huge benefit to anyone in any stage of the journey through making higher education possible. **Phyllis really nails it!"***

--Dale Zevenbergen, MBA, CPA, Professor of Business and Accounting

*"**Outstanding book that covers all aspects of making college affordable.** The online calculators allowed my children the opportunity to see exactly what they do now and during college can impact their future debt."*

--The Vacura Family with four college bound children

*"**After attending a workshop, my children commented 'WOW, MOM'.** I felt much more prepared for what we needed to do the next two years. I learned I was not prepared one bit and that the senior year is not the time to start this process. I did not realize there's so much to do to get ready for college. **I believe I would not be this far planning if it wasn't for College Survivor. "***

--The Hartman Family with two college bound children

Believe in Yourself!
You've Got This!

"College Survivor helped me win over $20,000 in scholarships."

--M.F., senior in high school

College Survivor is Written from a Mom and Student Perspective

Dear *College Survivors,*

Our family has the same fears as most families about the escalating cost of college. But we do not allow fear to crush our dreams. Not today and not tomorrow! This book is written in real time. Each chapter is based on real events and real problems with real solutions. No hypotheticals.

The goal is to answer *where, what,* and *why* and offer the much-needed solution of *how.* Our family has learned from trial and error in trying to assist our high school children prepare for college. We learned the hard way. This book is designed to teach you the easier way. Turning dreams into goals. Goals into plans. Plans into results!

P. Solis-Friederich

You are invited to join our family as we prepare our children for

their college journey—DEBT FREE!

CONTENTS

Quick Read

Chapter	Question	Parents	High School	College
1	*What is College Survivor Strategy and how can it help me?*	*Parents*	*High School*	*College*
2	*What are the common myths about scholarships and how are they busted?*	*Parents*	*High School*	*College*
3	*Tony and Tina learn about the financial impact of their decisions and face reality.*	*Parents*	*High School*	*College*
4	*The Smiths vs. the Jones College Planning vs. Waiting*	*Parents*		
5	*What is a scholarship, grant, loan, work study? Where do I start?*	*Parents*	*High School*	*College*
6	*What are the best tips for saving money and stretching the dollar while in college?*		*High School*	*College*
7	*How do priorities get mixed up? Food, shelter, and transportation.*		*High School*	*College*
8	*How do various generations think and act? How do both communicate?*	*Parents*		
9	*How do you mentor a college-bound child? Tips and stories.*	*Parents*		
10	*What can I do to assist my child to prepare for college while in high school?*	*Parents*	*High School*	
11	*What do I do if? Numerous scenarios for parents/children or mentors/students.*	*Parents*	*High School*	*College*
12	*Do you have a balanced life? Are you stressed? Learn techniques.*		*High School*	*College*
13	*Is there power in numbers? Why are teams so successful?*	*Parents*	*High School*	*College*
14	*How can I help my child with step one of College Survivor Strategy?*	*Parents*		
15	*What is the S.T.A.R. Method? How does it work? How can it help me?*	*Parents*	*High School*	*College*
16	*What are some great tips for a new career and future?*			*College*
17	*What are my online tools at www.collegesurvivorbook.com?*	*Parents*	*High School*	*College*
18	*What is the history of College Survivor and information about the author?*	*Parents*	*High School*	*College*

"One of my greatest mentors taught me not to worry about time and payout. His philosophy was that if you dedicate your time for the right reason, money will find you. And his strategy was right."

P. Solis-Friederich, the corporate rookie

CHAPTER 1
STRATEGY
THE MISSING LINK

> *"Strategy is a Commodity,*
> *Execution is an Art"*
> *Peter Drucker*

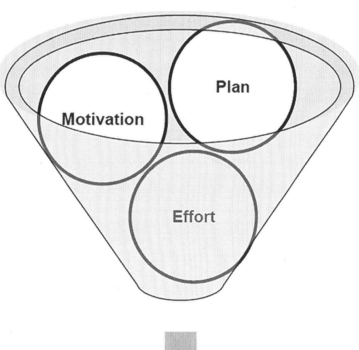

The *College Survivor*

College Survivor is the **name** of this book.

College Survivor Strategy is the **heart** of this book (chapter 15)

College Survivor

Began With a Little White Bag

Dear *College Survivor*,

It all started with a little white bag that our family received after attending a high school college night. Inside was pure gold. Tucked away in this bag was incredible information that provided *where, when*, and *why*… but not *how*.

This little white bag sat in the corner of our living room for months, just collecting dust.

As a parent, I sat frustrated with such gold and had not a thought of how to use it. So, I began to research. Hours became days and days became months. A folder became a three-ring binder, and research evolved into a plan. Shortly after, my children's friends began to ask if I could help them too. And then… *College Survivor* was born.

The gold just needed a STRATEGY.

"*How*" was the missing link and the solution!

This is why *College Survivor* is so different than other resources! Not only will this book guide you on your college journey, but you will have additional support on **www.CollegeSurvivorBook.com** and **The University of Success**.

College Survivor is here to help you determine your **Situation**.

Then assist you in developing your plan. **Task**.

We will teach you how to execute your plan. **Action**.

And, finally, we will guide you to evaluate your **Results**.

The goal of *College Survivor* is to help you. You are not alone!

P. Solis-Friederich, the researching mom

In This Chapter

1. What is *College Survivor Strategy?*

   a. S.T.A.R. Method

   b. Dream Team

2. What is *College Survivor,* the book and E-book

3. Website description

4. What is University of Success?

5. How is *College Survivor* different than other resources?

6. What is expected for my TIME and PAYOUT?

7. Who needs *College Survivor*?

What is *College Survivor Strategy*?

College Survivor Strategy is a cyclical process that assists parents and students to develop dreams into goals by designing a plan of execution. The concept uses the S.T.A.R. (situation, task, action, result) method in conjunction with the team method, a.k.a. the *"Dream Team,"* a real concept.

S.T.A.R. Method

Situation: this is your current situation and your financial gap.

Task: this is your plan of execution.

Action: this is *how* you execute your plan.

Results: this is the prize—your scholarships!

Then, repeat.

Dream Team

Every mega machine needs perfectly designed parts to function properly. You are no different. *College Survivor Strategy* is designed for a team of students or parents. The beauty of a team is that there is a higher chance of success. It can be quite lonely taking on a project by yourself. A teammate can be the motivating force to keep the machine working successfully.

There are four members of a Dream Team. Each team member has a different role that is important to the plan.

The CEO

The CEO plays the role of visionary and leader.

The Idea Guru

The Idea Guru has a natural talent for creating new ideas and different ways of doing things and can bring a breath of fresh air to the team.

The Communication Specialist

The Communication Specialist naturally wants to make sure everyone is up to date with what's going on with the project.

The Analyst

The Analyst is the problem solver. They can see solutions.

What is *College Survivor*, The Book and E-Book?

College Survivor is a user guide for college scholarships and grants. The heart of the book is *College Survivor Strategy*, the *how* – chapter 15, page 139.

Website

www.CollegeSurvivorBook.com supports each chapter with teaching videos. The series of videos provide added information that is not available in the book. In addition, the website provides customized tools to support the philosophy of the book.

Free (public) information is provided, which is available online or in bookstores. The purpose is to save you time by providing critical information in one location. We have completed the research to save you time.

Examples of free information include the following:

❖ Link to federal aid information (FAFSA)
❖ Links to state information
❖ Links to supplemental videos
❖ Links to unique scholarships
❖ *College Survivor* Humanitarian Program
❖ *College Survivor* scholarships, contests, drawings, and competitions
❖ And much more!

University of Success

The University of Success is available on our website www.CollegeSurvivorBook.com.

It is designed for those who are following *College Survivor Strategy,* either individually or as a Dream Team. All materials support *College Survivor Strategy,* plus provide added customized tools and features.

University of Success is like a book that has come to life, with new video series, interviews, and programs. This section of our website is an extension of *College Survivor,* the book and e-book!

University of Success also offers several opportunities for contests, drawings, and competitions, from Kindergarten to Graduate School. A percentage of every sold book, product, and service is set aside to fund these programs. The more sold, the higher the value of the contest, drawing, and competition, and the more opportunities available. Opportunities are updated annually.

College Survivor scholarships, contests, drawings, and competitions are not merit (GPA), financial need, or ethnic background-based. All programs are designed to be fair and equivalent without segregation. So, you may find that we judge based on effort, character, passion, and good old-fashioned work ethic. *College Survivor* is committed to rewarding students for excellence!

University of Success includes:

(Reference: Chapter 17)

- ❖ Documents
  - Parent/Student Commitment Contract
  - What if Role Play
  - Scams/Identity Theft Alert
  - Roommate Contract Terms and Conflict Resolution
- ❖ Checklists
  - Off to College (Dorm, First Apartment)
- ❖ Questions (Academic/Financial)
  - High School and College
- ❖ Academic Tips
  - Power of the Transcript, Final Exam Preparation, Low GPA Strategy

- ❖ Single Parents
  - Tips and advice
- ❖ Calculators
  - Savings in a Jar Calculator
  - Employment Calculator (HS and College)
  - Financial Deficit Calculator
  - Scholarship Deficit Calculator
- ❖ Best Scholarship/Grant Websites
- ❖ Best-Selling Books
  - ACT prep, college search, scholarship listings, and more
- ❖ Best Apps
  - Budgeting, time management, class assignments and more
- ❖ Chapter Videos
  - Videos and demonstrations that support each chapter of this book
  - Videos and demonstrations of new chapters not included in this book

How is *College Survivor* different than other resources?

The resources in today's market are excellent. They provide the *where, when,* and *why,* but not the *how. College Survivor Strategy* provides the missing link. *College Survivor Strategy* teaches you *how* by coaching you step-by-step through the process. You are no longer alone trying to find, organize, apply, and manage your scholarship applications.

What is expected for my Time and Payout?

The Time and Payout Matrix is designed for any parent or student Dream Team planning to assemble and meet on a regular basis. The purpose is to help teams understand the recommended number of meetings, time commitment, scholarship applications, and the payout for the effort. The following example is a recommendation, and the payout results are an estimate. The payout depends on when you start *College Survivor Strategy,* how long you continue, and your rate of return.

How much time does it take to apply for a scholarship?

- ❖ Elementary and middle school: application time varies. 30 min to 1 hour.

- ❖ 8th grade: application time average is 1 hour to 1 hour and 45 minutes.

- ❖ High school: application time average is 1 hour 45 minutes.

- ❖ College: application time average is 1 hour and 45 minutes.

What is the Payout?

- ❖ six years of elementary = $4,860 / $45 per hour

- ❖ three years of middle school = $6,720 / $80 per hour

- ❖ four years of high school = $43,200 / $94 per hour

- ❖ four years of college = $64,800 / $113 per hour

Time and Payout Matrix
College Survivor Strategy

Level	Meetings		HOURS			Scholarship Information				Payout	
Grade	Meet per Mo.	Meet per yr.	Min. Hrs. per mtg.	Max Hrs. per mtg.	Ttl. Hrs. per yr.	# Schol. App. Per mtg.	# Schol. App. Per yr.	Ave. Schol. $ per App.	Ttl. Schol. $ per yr.	20% payout	Pay per max hr.
K		4	2	4	16	3	12	$250	$3,000	$600	$38
1		4	2	4	16	3	12	$250	$3,000	$600	$38
2		4	2	4	16	3	12	$250	$3,000	$600	$38
3		4	2	4	16	3	12	$250	$3,000	$600	$38
4		4	2	4	16	3	12	$350	$4,200	$840	$53
5		6	2	4	24	3	18	$450	$8,100	$1,620	$68
Elementary School Totals:									$24,300	$4,860	$45
6		6	3	4	24	3	18	$500	$9,000	$1,800	$75
7		7	3	4	28	3	21	$600	$12,600	$2,520	$90
8		8	3	4	32	2	16	$750	$12,000	$2,400	$75
Middle School Totals:									$33,600	$6,720	$80
9	1	12	3	4	48	2	24	$750	$18,000	$3,600	$75
10	2	24	3	4	96	2	48	$750	$36,000	$7,200	$75
11	3	36	3	4	144	2	72	$750	$81,000	$16,200	$113
12	3	36	3	4	144	2	72	$750	$81,000	$16,200	$113
High School Totals:									$216,000	$43,200	$94
FR	3	36	3	4	144	2	72	$750	$81,000	$16,200	$113
So	3	36	3	4	144	2	72	$750	$81,000	$16,200	$113
Jr	3	36	3	4	144	2	72	$750	$81,000	$16,200	$113
Sr	3	36	3	4	144	2	72	$750	$81,000	$16,200	$113
College Totals:									$324,000	$64,800	$113
									$597,900	$119,580	

Estimates are based on following College Survivor Strategy, chapter 15, page 139.

In some cases, a student may not be able to work or chooses to become a scholarship application specialist. In such cases, the following example would apply.

Time and Payout Matrix
No Employment

Level	Meetings		HOURS			Scholarship Information				Payout	
College	Meet per Mo.	Meet Per Yr.	Min Hrs. Per Mtg.	Max Hrs. Per Mtg	Ttl Hrs. Per Yr. (max)	# Schol App Per Mtg	# Schol App Per Yr.	Ave. Schol $ per App	Ttl Scholar $ Per Yr.	20% Pay	Pay per Max Hr.
FR	6	72	3.5	4.5	324	3	216	$750	$162,500	$32,500	$120
So	6	72	3.5	4.5	324	3	216	$750	$162,500	$32,500	$120
Jr	6	72	3.5	4.5	324	3	216	$750	$162,500	$32,500	$120
Sr	6	72	3.5	4.5	324	3	216	$750	$162,500	$32,500	$120
College Totals:									$650,000	$130,000	$120

Estimates are based on following College Survivor Strategy, chapter 15, page 139.

In the above example, this student would meet with his/her Dream Team twice per week – three times per month for twelve months. This scenario is an alternative to *College Survivor Strategy.* This student would commit to applying for scholarships approximately 7 to 9 hours per week in lieu of employment. The above example is an estimate and based on winning 20% of scholarship applications.

Is this possible? Can a student commit to a full time job of applying for scholarships twice a week? This situation is possible if the student is able to find over 200 annual scholarships of which they are qualified. A determined student may be able to accomplish this task. *College Survivor Strategy* is more realistic and attainable. This example serves as an alternative for students with employment limitations.

Explanation of Categories (Time and Payout Matrix)

Level: academic level of the student.

Meetings: suggested meetings per month, year, and academic level.

Hours: suggested minimum and maximum meeting hours by month, year, and academic level.

Scholarship Information: recommended number of scholarship applications by month, year, and academic level. Also, an estimate of scholarship dollars per application, per year.

Payout: an estimate of payout based on 100% effort and 20% payout with estimate of earnings per hour of effort.

Explanation of Terms (Time and Payout Matrix)

➢ Meet per Mo. = Meetings per Month

    • Suggested meeting times per month for your Dream Team. If the column is blank, your Dream Team does not meet monthly. Refer to the meetings per year.

➢ Meet per Yr. = Meetings Per Year

    • Suggested meeting times per year for your Dream Team.

➢ Min. Hrs. per Mtg. = Minimum Hours Per Meeting

    • Suggested minimum hours per meeting for your Dream Team.

➢ Max Hrs. per mtg. = Maximum Hours Per. Meeting

    • Suggested maximum hours per meeting for your Dream Team.

➢ Ttl. Hrs. per Yr. (Max) = Total Hours Per Year, Maximum

    • Total suggested number of hours that your Dream Team should spend in meetings in one year (at the maximum level).

➢ # Schol. App. Per Mtg. = Number of Scholarship Applications Per Meeting

    • Suggested number of scholarships applications per month. This is your individual scholarship application goal.

➢ # Schol. App. Per Yr. = Number of Scholarship Applications Per Year

    • An estimate of the total number of scholarships that your student should apply for in a 12-month period.

➢ Ave. Schol. $ per App. = Average Scholarship Dollars Per Scholarship Application

    • An estimate of the total amount of dollars that your student should apply for in a 12-month period.

➢ Ttl. Scholar $ Per Yr. = Total Scholarship Dollar Applications per Year

    • An estimate of how many scholarship dollar applications in one year based on following the suggested schedule of meetings and scholarship applications.

➢ 20% Pay = 20% Payout for Effort

    • A financial estimate of the payout for your effort in a 12-month period based on following the suggested schedule of meetings and individual scholarship applications.

➢ Pay Per Max Hr. = Payout per Maximum Hour

* A financial estimate of the payout per hour for your effort in one year based on following the suggested schedule of meetings and individual scholarship applications.

Who Needs *College Survivor*?

❖ Parents of students kindergarten to graduate school and beyond

❖ High school students

❖ Under graduate and graduate students

❖ Trade school students

❖ Single parents and returning adults

❖ Anyone with hopes and dreams who does not know how to develop a plan to make their dreams a reality!

Elementary School Students (Parents)

Most parents do not even consider the fact that there are scholarships, contests, and drawings for students as early as kindergarten. It is hard to imagine that these tots were just out of diapers and now a parent can actually apply for a scholarship. Well, it is true. Tip: Next time you are in a large bookstore, go to the college section and open a digest of scholarship listings. Just take a minute to look at general scholarships, drawings, and contests, and you will quickly find that there are numerous opportunities starting at kindergarten.

Middle School Students (Parents)

Age 13 is the "green light go" age. This should be around eighth grade. Scholarships become more abundant starting at this age. As a parent, if you have not started a parent Dream Team (refer to chapter 13), now is the time! Eighth grade is busy, just like any year, but the eighth grade year is a great year to start practicing *College Survivor Strategy*. This way, when your student begins high school, your family will have a year's worth of practice. The first year is the hardest because of the learning curve. Learn and practice before high school begins so you will be a PRO. By the time your student is a senior in high school, they should be well-funded to start college.

High School (Parents and Students)

The sooner you are able to begin *College Survivor Strategy*, the better! It is never too late. Most parents and students have the impression that applying for scholarships begins the senior year. This is untrue. If you were to pick the most critical time to begin the scholarship application process, it would be the summer after the sophomore year, or at very latest, the summer after the junior year. Waiting till the senior year will eliminate the opportunity for at least 50% of scholarships. Many parents may think they waited too long and there are no longer any scholarships available. In reality, there are scholarships every day of the year. Just start as soon as possible to gain momentum.

College and Trade School Students

Start today. Even if you have outstanding loans, you may be able to earn enough scholarships to pay for the loans. Follow *College Survivor Strategy* with a more aggressive approach and you will soon see the payout for your efforts.

"30 years from Now,

It won't matter what Shoes you wore,

How your Hair looked or the Jeans you bought.

What will matter is...

What you Learned and How you Used It."

- Anonymous

Resources available at
www.CollegeSurvivorBook.com / University of Success section!
Remember! Believe in Yourself! You've Got This!

"When I first began to research college information, I was curious if my own perceptions were true or false. I found that I had preconceived notions that were false. It was such a relief to read various studies and statistics that busted these myths!"

P. Solis-Friederich, the curious researching mom

CHAPTER 2
MYTHS AND MISCONCEPTIONS
PERCEPTION VS. REALITY

> *"Thoughts become perceptions,*
> *Perceptions become reality.*
> *Alter your thoughts, alter your reality."*
> *--William James*

In this Chapter

1. Perception vs. reality

2. Top seven myths

A perception is something we think. It is emotionally driven. We have either been given information and assume our own opinion, or we have been conditioned to think a specific way. The interesting thing is that our thoughts, entwined with our emotions and all the incredible dynamics of the neurotransmitters (in our brain), send signals here and there to create our reality.

Once we have determined our reality, it is a battle to rethink, or reboot our brain, and create a new reality. It is not impossible, but certainly a process. While researching the most common myths and misconceptions about scholarships, my eyes were opened as a former student, and now a mentor of my children. Surveys, statistical data, and research papers provided scores of percentages, opinions, and evaluation of data. The important thing to know is that, despite differing numerical statistics and percentages, all the sources I researched consistently had the same end-result. The results are incredible and give hope to all students and parents. I was personally relieved to read and study the statistics.

Knowing the truth, based on facts, changed my perception and internal fears as I approached scholarship program development for my children (which ultimately led to this book). In several of my workshops, I presented factual data that busted all the myths. At the end of sessions, I asked parents and students how they felt about the myth and misconception presentation, and the responses included words and phrases such as, "relieved," "feel so much better," "I have a chance," "made me feel less pressured," and "I feel less overwhelmed." Notice that all the verbs in the responses are emotional, which indicate a perception. The attendees of the workshops developed a new mindset in a short presentation. Ultimately, their new perception translated into turning their hopes and dreams into a reality. Then, we proceeded to turn their new realities into a realistic plan.

I must say, this is one of my favorite topics to present, because as I watch the body language and facial expressions of each attendee at the beginning of the myth presentation, I see doubt, despair, and even fear. After each myth is busted, I see a sparkle in their eyes, improved postures, and an increase in alertness. It is an incredible evolution of turning destructive myths (old perceptions) into positive and motivating realities.

Busting these myths is powerful and critical to the mindset. These myths are destructive and can diminish hope. The good news is that they are myths, and they are busted! Just exactly what are these myths? I chose my top seven, because these are the ones that raise eyebrows.

TOP SEVEN MYTHS AND MISCONCEPTIONS

Myth #1 Busted:
"I'm not a straight 'A' student.
Everyone knows all the scholarships go to students with the best grades."

Who really wins scholarships based on merit (GPA)?

- ❖ 52% GPA 3.4 to 4.0
- ❖ 30% GPA 2.9 to 3.3
- ❖ 09% GPA 2.5 to 2.8

It is evident that merit-based scholarships (grades) are awarded at a higher percentage to students with a higher GPA. But notice that scholarships are also awarded to students with a lower GPA. As I organized the 150 scholarships for my senior in high school, I found many scholarships have minimum requirements as low as a 2.0 GPA. This is great hope for the student with non-stellar grades. In addition, numerous scholarships do not even have a GPA requirement. Each scholarship is so different. Every rule and regulation is different. No two are alike. If you are talented in a special area, there are scholarships for you. If you volunteer your time, there are scholarships for you. I could list all the possibilities, but it would take pages and pages.

Never give up because of grades, but always strive to improve your GPA because it increases your odds of winning even more scholarships.

> ## Myth #2 Busted:
> "I'm not a minority.
> I have always heard that minorities receive the most money."

Who really wins scholarships based on ethnic background?

Here are the odds of winning:

13.9% Caucasian

11.1% Minority

11.3% African American

Well, take a look at the numbers. The statistics displayed are an average of 10 studies I found across the United States, from all demographic areas. I see hope and equality. All you need to do is apply. A scholarship is waiting for you. Conquer your fears! Whether your skin color is orange, purple, or blue... it does not matter!

> ## Myth #3 Busted:
> "Athletes seem to always get a full ride.
> There probably isn't any money left for non-athletes."

Who really wins scholarships based on athletics?

1.2% of athletic students receive scholarships.

$7,900 is the average scholarship, which is 33% of cost of attendance.

Athletic scholarships represent 5.3% of institutional grants and 2.2% of college grants.

If you are an athlete, you will desperately need assistance from *College Survivor Strategy*. As for the non-athletes, do the math! If athletics students are receiving 7.5% of grants (5.3 + 2.2%), that means 92.5% of grants are available to non-athletes. That is a lot of money. All you have to do is apply! *College Survivor Strategy* can and will help you!

Myth #4 Busted:
"Only high school seniors are eligible to apply for scholarships.
I guess I will wait 'til I am a senior."

Are scholarships only available for high school seniors?

Students can apply for scholarships at every grade level, starting in kindergarten. Scholarships, contests, drawings, and competitions are available every day of the year. Scholarships do not stop. They are even available for graduate students and doctorate students. Scholarship deadlines vary throughout every month of the year. *College Survivor Strategy* (Chapter 15) recommends scholarship review and application at least two months before the actual due date. This will give plenty of time to satisfy any special requirements for the scholarship foundation. Deadlines tend to peak in the fall and spring. A senior who waits until the spring of the senior year will miss about half the deadlines for seniors.

Keep in mind: The Children's Online Privacy Protection Act (COPPA) requires verifiable parental consent to collect information from children under age 13.

Myth #5 Busted:
"I'm not the valedictorian, and everyone knows they receive full rides.
I will have to work harder!"

Do all valedictorians receive a free ride?

Consider how many schools there are in the United States and the thousands of valedictorians. The answer is NO.

Who really wins scholarships?

.325% receive enough grants and scholarships to fund 100% of college costs.

1.25% receive enough grants and scholarships to fund 90% of college costs.

3.45% receive enough grants and scholarships to fund 75% of college costs.

14.3% receive enough grants and scholarships to fund 50% of college costs.

Valedictorians can graduate debt-free if they embrace *College Survivor Strategy*! In fact, this high-achieving student will most likely win more than enough scholarships to fund undergraduate, graduate, and postgraduate studies.

Myth #6 Busted:
"My parents make too much money.
All of the scholarship money goes to low income students."

Statistics stated below are income based on AGI (Adjusted Gross Income).

Who really wins scholarships based on income?

14.0% middle income ($50K to $100K)

10.9% low income (<$50K)

10.7% upper income (>$100K)

There are two ways to evaluate these findings. First, only 35.6% (14.0 + 10.9 + 10.7%) of scholarships are considered income-based. Notice how each income level is almost equivalent. Second, this leaves 64.4% of scholarships that do not require an income statement and rely on talent, merit, volunteer service, or character, and the list continues. 64.4% is a huge opportunity for students. So, this myth is completely busted.

Myth #7 Busted:
"I doubt there are scholarships for me.
I just do not have time, anyway."

Who really wins scholarships when they invest their time?

Winning can be skill-based (talent, volunteer, etc.)

Winning can be luck-based (drawings and contests)

Winning can be merit-based (grades)

Winning only happens if you apply

We just busted seven of the most common myths. At workshops and on our website, www. CollegeSurvivorBook.com, we reveal even more myths and misconceptions. The great thing about our website is that as new studies evolve and time passes, we can communicate the latest findings to you. And you are welcome to contact us if there is a myth (student fear) that has you concerned. We will research your concern and reply with a comprehensive answer, not only for you, but for all those who registered on our website.

It is our hope that after reading about the above seven myths, you will be more confident and all your old perceptions will have turned into new realties. Feeling great and confident is important. We believe in you! Now, just believe in yourself. The odds are in your favor. I know I felt better as a parent when I realized that. Even at the age of fifty-one, I had the very same fears as I did when I was younger. But my old perceptions are gone. I have new realities, and I am passing the torch to you. Conquer your fears! You can do it!

NOTES

Resources available at
www.CollegeSurvivorBook.com / University of Success section!
Remember! Believe in Yourself! You've Got This

"How do I budget? What will be the impact of my decisions? I still have my handwritten budget book from college. My dad taught me how to budget. I tracked every penny and had a plan for the week and the month. Did I veer from the plan? Yes, I am human, too!"

P. Solis-Friederich, the budgeting college student

CHAPTER 3
MONEY, MONEY
CASE STUDIES / IMPACT OF DECISIONS

> *"When your values are clear to you,*
> *making decisions becomes easier."*
> *--Roy E. Disney*

In This Chapter

1. Tony vs. Tina: two years of college

2. Tony vs. Tina: four years of college

3. Tony vs. Tina: the impact of their decisions

On the next several pages, you will see how different situations impact the pocketbook, and how planning and decisions unfold. We begin with two years in college and progress to four years of college, with different variables.

As each situation progresses, different components of *College Survivor Strategy* are added to show all the pros and cons of implementing a plan. At the end of this section, all the situations are pulled together for a reality check.

Tony vs. Tina

Tony. He has decided to pursue a four-year degree with a plan of attending a community college for two years, then transferring to a four-year university.

Tina. She has decided to pursue a four-year degree with a plan of entering the university her freshman year and staying all four years until graduation.

Both will live in the dorm during their entire college career. Books and fees are included in the the cost of their education. Personal vehicle, gas, upkeep, and vehicle insurance are not included.

No Employment	No Financial Assistance	No *College Survivor*	DEBT

Two Years of College

Scenario #1: Tony and Tina decided to not continue their education beyond two years. Tony did graduate with a two-year degree, but Tina dropped out. Both lived in the dorm. Transportation was provided by their parents. In this situation, Tony and Tina did not work or apply for financial assistance, and they also did not apply for any scholarships. The result? They owe money to pay back loans. At least Tony has a two-year degree. Tina will struggle as a dropout.

EFFORT

Tony	Education Cost*	Tina	Education Cost*
Year 1 *Community College*	$16,432.45	**Year 1** *University*	$32,864.90
Year 2 *Community College*	$16,432.45	**Year 2** *University*	$32,864.90
Total Owed	**$32,864.90**	**Total Owed**	**$65,729.80**

Education Cost based on average cost of an education in the United States. Included is tuition, fees, books and cost of living. Not included is personal vehicle.

RESULT

Tony	Monthly Payment*	Tina	Monthly Payment*
5 yr. / 60 mo.	$547.75	5 yr. loan / 60 mo.	$1,095.50
10 yr. / 120 mo.	$273.87	10 yr. loan / 120 mo.	$547.75
15 yr. / 180 mo.	$182.58	15 yr. loan / 180 mo.	$365.17

Monthly payment does not include interest.

| No Employment | No Financial Assistance | No *College Survivor* | HUGE DEBT |

Four Years of College

Scenario #2: Tony and Tina completed their four years of education. Both lived in the dorm all four years. Transportation was provided by their parents. In this situation, they did not work or apply for financial assistance and they also did not apply for any scholarships. The result? They owe money to pay back loans. They both have four-year degrees but will endure hefty payments per month. They may have to move back home for five years to pay this debt, and possibly work a second job to eliminate the debt faster. This debt will delay progress with buying a home and upgrading cars. They may have a new home in the basement at their parents' house.

EFFORT

Tony	Education Cost*	Tina	Education Cost*
Year 1 Community College	$16,432.45	**Year 1** University	$32,864.90
Year 2 Community College	$16,432.45	**Year 2** University	$32,864.90
Year 3 University	$32,864.90	**Year 3** University	$32,864.90
Year 4 University	$32,864.90	**Year 4** University	$32,864.90
Total Owed	**$98,594.70**	**Total Owed**	**$131,459.60**

Education Cost based on average cost of an education in the United States. Included is tuition, fees, books and cost of living. Not included is personal vehicle.

RESULT

Tony	Monthly Payment*	Tina	Monthly Payment*
5 yr. / 60 mo.	$1,643.25	5 yr. loan / 60 mo.	$2,190.99
10 yr. / 120 mo.	$821.62	10 yr. loan / 120 mo.	$1,095.50
15 yr. / 180 mo.	$547.75	15 yr. loan / 180 mo.	$730.33

Monthly payment does not include interest.

Four Years of College + $20,000 HS Scholarship

<u>Scenario #3:</u> Tony and Tina both received substantial scholarships in high school—$20,000 is a lot of money. But, they did not plan by determining their financial deficit and devising a plan to close the financial deficit (gap). This will be a very costly decision. Time and effort could have impacted the end result. Now, both will begin their new careers with a big debt. This will impact the opportunity to invest discretionary income in retirement, purchase a home, and upgrade vehicles.

EFFORT

Tony	Education Cost*	Tina	Education Cost*
Year 1 *Community College*	$16,432.45	**Year 1** *University*	$32,864.90
Year 2 *Community College*	$16,432.45	**Year 2** *University*	$32,864.90
Year 3 *University*	$32,864.90	**Year 3** *University*	$32,864.90
Year 4 *University*	$32,864.90	**Year 4** *University*	$32,864.90
High School Scholarship	-$20,000.00	*High School Scholarship*	-$20,000.00
Total Owed	**$78,594.70**	**Total Owed**	**$111,459.60**

Education Cost based on average cost of an education in the United States. Included is tuition, fees, books and cost of living. Not included is personal vehicle.

RESULT

Tony	Monthly Payment*	Tina	Monthly Payment*
5 yr. / 60 mo.	$1,309.91	5 yr. loan / 60 mo.	$1,857.66
10 yr. / 120 mo.	$654.96	10 yr. loan / 120 mo.	$928.83
15 yr. / 180 mo.	$436.64	15 yr. loan / 180 mo.	$619.22

Monthly payment does not include interest.

Tony and Tina's Decision – Plan A

Tony and Tina are feeling discouraged because they realize that $20,000.00 in scholarships from high school is not enough. They begin to utilize the tools available at www.CollegeSurvivorBook.com in the University of Success section. They test the various calculators and devise a plan. Their first plan is to not work, just live smart poor. The planning process begins.

EFFORT

Tony	Education Cost*	Tina	Education Cost*
Year 1 *Community College*	$16,432.45	**Year 1** *University*	$32,864.90
Year 2 *Community College*	$16,432.45	**Year 2** *University*	$32,864.90
Year 3 *University*	$32,864.90	**Year 3** *University*	$32,864.90
Year 4 *University*	$32,864.90	**Year 4** *University*	$32,864.90
High School Scholarship	-$20,000.00	*High School Scholarship*	-$20,000.00
Smart Poor** *(10% reduction living cost)*	-$9,859.47	*Smart Poor*** *(10% reduction living cost)*	-$13,145.96
Total Owed	**$68,735.23**	**Total Owed**	**$98,313.64**

Education Cost based on average cost of an education in the United States. Included is tuition, fees, books and cost of living. Not included is personal vehicle. **Silly Rich vs. Smart Poor, Chapter 6, page 53.

RESULT

Tony	Monthly Payment*	Tina	Monthly Payment*
5 yr. / 60 mo.	$1,145.59	5 yr. loan / 60 mo.	$1,638.56
10 yr. / 120 mo.	$572.79	10 yr. loan / 120 mo.	$819.28
15 yr. / 180 mo.	$381.86	15 yr. loan / 180 mo.	$546.19

Monthly payment does not include interest.

Decision Results

Well, hats off to saving money! But there is a substantial gap despite the efforts of living smart poor. Once again, Tony and Tina are disappointed and begin devising a new plan.

| College Paycheck Only | Plan B |

Tony and Tina's Decision – Plan B

Tony and Tina invent a new plan. They decide to work and forget the smart poor strategy. Certainly, they will make enough money!

EFFORT

Tony	Education Cost*	Tina	Education Cost*
Year 1 *Community College*	$16,432.45	**Year 1** *University*	$32,864.90
Year 2 *Community College*	$16,432.45	**Year 2** *University*	$32,864.90
Year 3 *University*	$32,864.90	**Year 3** *University*	$32,864.90
Year 4 *University*	$32,864.90	**Year 4** *University*	$32,864.90
High School Scholarship	-$20,000.00	*High School Scholarship*	-$20,000.00
College Paycheck ***	-$46,285.20	*College Paycheck****	-$46,285.20
Total Owed	**$32,309.50**	**Total Owed**	**$65,174.40**

*Education Cost based on average cost of an education in the United States. Included is tuition, fees, books and cost of living. Not included is personal vehicle. ***College Paycheck, 4 years, major store, chapter 15, page 146.

RESULT

Tony	Monthly Payment*	Tina	Monthly Payment*
5 yr. / 60 mo.	$538.49	5 yr. loan / 60 mo.	$1,086.24
10 yr. / 120 mo.	$269.25	10 yr. loan / 120 mo.	$543.12
15 yr. / 180 mo.	$179.50	15 yr. loan / 180 mo.	$362.08

*Monthly payment does not include interest.

Decision results

Still not enough! Many students will overwork, and so begins the domino effect of sleep deprivation and countless issues.

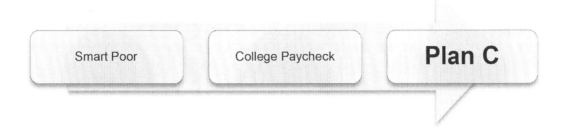

Tony and Tina's Decision – Plan C

Tony and Tina then devise a plan C. Tony and Tina think, "*We will work and live smart poor, and we should have it made!*"

EFFORT

Tony	Education Cost*	Tina	Education Cost*
Year 1 *Community College*	$16,432.45	**Year 1** *University*	$32,864.90
Year 2 *Community College*	$16,432.45	**Year 2** *University*	$32,864.90
Year 3 *University*	$32,864.90	**Year 3** *University*	$32,864.90
Year 4 *University*	$32,864.90	**Year 4** *University*	$32,864.90
High School Scholarship	-$20,000.00	*High School Scholarship*	-$20,000.00
*Smart Poor*** *(10% reduction living cost)*	-$9,859.47	*Smart Poor*** *(10% reduction living cost)*	-$13,145.96
*College Paycheck****	-$46,285.20	*College Paycheck****	-$46,285.20
Total Owed	**$22,450.03**	**Total Owed**	**$52,028.44**

*Education Cost based on average cost of an education in the United States. Included is tuition, fees, books and cost of living. Not included is personal vehicle. **Silly Rich vs. Smart Poor, Chapter 6, page 53. ***College Paycheck, 4 years, major store, chapter 15, page 146.

RESULT

Tony	Monthly Payment*	Tina	Monthly Payment*
5 yr. / 60 mo.	$374.17	5 yr. loan / 60 mo.	$867.14
10 yr. / 120 mo.	$187.08	10 yr. loan / 120 mo.	$433.57
15 yr. / 180 mo.	$124.72	15 yr. loan / 180 mo.	$289.05

*Monthly payment does not include interest.

Decision Results

Still not enough money, but much closer to the goal. Tony and Tina begin the process of developing Plan D.

Tony and Tina's Decision – Plan D

Tony and Tina agree on a plan D. Both agree to assemble a Dream Team (Chapter 13) and follow *College Survivor Strategy* for earning scholarships (Chapter 15).

EFFORT

Tony	Education Cost*	Tina	Education Cost*
Year 1 *Community College*	$16,432.45	**Year 1** *University*	$32,864.90
Year 2 *Community College*	$16,432.45	**Year 2** *University*	$32,864.90
Year 3 *University*	$32,864.90	**Year 3** *University*	$32,864.90
Year 4 *University*	$32,864.90	**Year 4** *University*	$32,864.90
High School Scholarship	-$20,000.00	*High School Scholarship*	-$20,000.00
*Smart Poor*** *(10% reduction living cost)*	-$9,859.47	*Smart Poor*** *(10% reduction living cost)*	-$13,145.96
*College Paycheck****	-$46,285.20	*College Paycheck****	-$46,285.20
*College Survivor Strategy Scholarships*****	-$53,000.00	*College Survivor Strategy Scholarships*****	-$53,000.00
Savings	**$30,549.97**	**Savings**	**$971.56**

*Education Cost based on average cost of an education in the United States. Included is tuition, fees, books and cost of living. Not included is personal vehicle. **Silly Rich vs. Smart Poor, chapter 6, page 53. ***College Paycheck, 4 years, major store, chapter 15, page 130.****College Survivor Strategy, chapter 15, page 146.

RESULT

Tony	Monthly Payment*	Tina	Monthly Payment*
5 yr. / 60 mo.	$0	5 yr. loan / 60 mo.	$0
10 yr. / 120 mo.	$0	10 yr. loan / 120 mo.	$0
15 yr. / 180 mo.	$0	15 yr. loan / 180 mo.	$0

*Monthly payment does not include interest

Decision Results

They both use the tools on www.CollegeSurvivorBook.com in the University of Success section and utilize the most important tool—The Scholarship Deficit Calculator. Tina enters her information and the calculator provides options to close the financial gap.

The Scholarship Deficit Calculator provides three options for Tina:

Average value of each scholarship application = $750

Option #1

Meet with Dream Team four times per month for 3.2 hours per meeting and apply for two individual scholarships per meeting.

Option #2

Meet with Dream Team three times per month for 4.2 hours per meeting and apply for three individual scholarships per meeting.

Option #3

Meet with Dream Team two times per month for 6.3 hours per meeting and apply for four individual scholarships per meeting.

The Scholarship Deficit Calculator provides three options for Tony that are less time-consuming. He decides to follow Tina's plan and support her so that she is not alone working on scholarship applications. A real team!

Teamwork

Tony stands by his friend Tina, and even though he does not need as much money as Tina, he follows her plan. Both are *College Survivors*. Tony and Tina graduate debt-free. Tina is headed off to begin her career, and Tony is headed to graduate school because he has money remaining at the university and a great opportunity to fund an even higher education.

Four Years of College + *College Survivor* with a Twist!

This scenario provides a twist. Tony and Tina have been provided a free ride for tuition, fees, and room and board by their college, and their parents are paying the car expenses. However, the parents declare that Tony and Tina must work if they want assistance with the car. Tony reads College Survivor (the book) and convinces Tina to join his Dream Team. Tony and Tina see the value *College Survivor Strategy* and embrace the process. They both live frugally (smart poor) and save their parents 10% of extra living expenses. They work and apply for scholarships following *College Survivor Strategy*. The result provides an opportunity for Tony and Tina to pursue graduate school, a dream that they thought was not possible.

EFFORT

Tony	Education Cost*	Tina	Education Cost*
4 Years of College	$0.00	**4 Years of College**	$0.00
College Paycheck***	$46,285.20	College Paycheck***	$46,285.20
College Survivor Strategy Scholarships****	$53,000.00	College Survivor Strategy Scholarships****	$53,000.00
Savings	**$99,285.20**	**Savings**	**$99,285.20**

*Education Cost, full ride example***College Paycheck, 4 years, major store, chapter 15, page 131.****College Survivor Strategy, Chapter 15, page 146.*

RESULT

Tony	Monthly Payment*	Tina	Monthly Payment*
5 yr. / 60 mo.	$0	5 yr. loan / 60 mo.	$0
10 yr. / 120 mo.	$0	10 yr. loan / 120 mo.	$0
15 yr. / 180 mo.	$0	15 yr. loan / 180 mo.	$0

Monthly payment does not include interest

THINKING OUTSIDE THE BOX

Is this possible? If you had everything paid for, would you even bother to work or apply for scholarships? Well, it does not take a math major to see that these two are the highest paid professional scholarship application gurus. Now that they can fund a master's degree, their future income just increased by thousands of dollars. And a dream they thought was just a wish can now become a reality. Their effort paid off! The above case studies can be very eye-opening, and they are a true indication of how decisions can impact the pocketbook upon graduation.

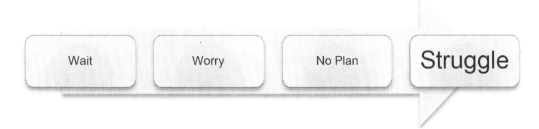

Reality Check

Many students decide to worry about it later, while others constantly worry but do not have a plan. When you worry about it later, you have to work harder. For example: in scenario #2, page 25. Tina did not work or apply for assistance. She lived completely on loans. She now owes $131,459.60 without interest.

What does this mean? How can a little planning and work payoff? Let's say Tina lands an incredible job, but she cannot afford her rent because of her college loans.

There are a couple ways Tina can pay these loans:

1. Tina can move home for five to eight years and use her new income to pay for the loan.

2. Tina can live on her own with her new job and take on a second job on the weekends to pay for the college debt.

3. **Tina can work as a waitress with a wage of $15 per hour. She would need to work every Saturday and Sunday (seven-hour shifts) for approximately 12 years. Additional years would be required for the interest on the loan.**

And how does the story end?

Wait for it! Wait for it....

Tony buys his parents a new car,

gives them a hug, and says, "Thank you!"

Now that's a great ending to a story!

Resources available at
www.CollegeSurvivorBook.com / University of Success section!
Remember! Believe in Yourself! You've Got This!

"If I had known about the 529 Plan when my kids were born, we would have thousands of dollars sitting in the bank for their future education. Now, without a dime in savings because of our medical bills, we are reliant on College Survivor Strategy. This will only cost us time and energy. I am okay with that!"

P. Solis-Friederich, a strategic mom

CHAPTER 4
THE SAVING PARENT
FINANCIAL STRATEGIES START EARLY

"Don't save what is left after spending,
but spend what is left after saving."
--Warren Buffet

In This Chapter

1. Saving in a jar: the power of the $20 bill

2. How do parents really pay for college?

3. The 529 Plan

   a. The Smith family vs. the Jones family

Saving money can be hard for some and easy for others. The power of the almighty dollar can be quite astounding. When something is out of sight, it is out of mind. Most banking institutions have Christmas accounts, vacation accounts, and college savings accounts, and the list continues. Your bank can take money straight out of your weekly or monthly paycheck. This allows the bank to manage the discipline of saving for you. Allow your hard-earned dollars to work for you rather than against you. When invested properly, your dollars can grow exponentially!

How Do Parents Really Pay for College?

There are numerous statistics and reviews regarding how parents really pay for college. Here is an average of six reliable sources. Keep in mind that statistics change every year as costs of education and costs of living increase. This is a good estimate of how parents pay across the United States. Below is the average amount borrowed as of 2016.

Parents Borrow:

- ❖ Private Education Loans: $10,572

- ❖ Other Loans: $10,257

- ❖ Federal Plus Loans: $10,114

- ❖ Home Equity Loans (HELOCs): $9,998

- ❖ Retirement Account Loans: $5,758

- ❖ Credit Cards: $2,863

Parents Use Their Own Funds:

- ❖ College Savings Plans (529): $9,236

- ❖ Retirement Savings Plans: $9,140

- ❖ Current Income: $7,809

- ❖ Other Savings Accounts: $6,340

As you can see, parents will find a way to assist their children in financing their college dreams. Sometimes the method is not the most advantageous to the family, but parents find a way.

SAVING IN A JAR
The Power of the $20 Bill

Below is a simple example of saving dollars in a jar without interest. The purpose is to show the impact of a $20 bill. The information below is for demonstration purposes only. Investing in a 529 plan will increase your investment and is highly recommended.

Start Saving Age	Grade	#yrs.	$ per week	Total $ saved	$ per week	Total $ saved
1		21	$20.00	$21,840	$10.00	$10,920
2		20	$20.00	$20,800	$10.00	$10,400
3		19	$20.00	$19,760	$10.00	$9,880
4		18	$20.00	$18,720	$10.00	$9,360
5		17	$20.00	$17,680	$10.00	$8,840
6	1	16	$20.00	$16,640	$10.00	$8,320
7	2	15	$20.00	$15,600	$10.00	$7,800
8	3	14	$20.00	$14,560	$10.00	$7,280
9	4	13	$20.00	$13,520	$10.00	$6,760
10	5	12	$20.00	$12,480	$10.00	$6,240
11	6	11	$20.00	$11,440	$10.00	$5,720
12	7	10	$20.00	$10,400	$10.00	$5,200
13	8	9	$20.00	$9,360	$10.00	$4,680
14	9	8	$20.00	$8,320	$10.00	$4,160
15	10	7	$20.00	$7,280	$10.00	$3,640
16	11	6	$20.00	$6,240	$10.00	$3,120
17	12	5	$20.00	$5,200	$10.00	$2,600
18	Fr/Coll	4	$20.00	$4,160	$10.00	$2,080
19	Soph/Coll	3	$20.00	$3,120	$10.00	$1,560
20	Jr/Coll	2	$20.00	$2,080	$10.00	$1,040
21	Sr/Coll	1	$20.00	$1,040	$10.00	$520

The 529 Plan

A 529 Plan is a type of investment account you can use to save for higher education. This plan is usually sponsored by states. This plan specifies certain tax advantages and originates from Section 529 of the Internal Revenue Code. Anyone can open a 529 plan—parents, grandparents, friends, and relatives. When you are an account owner, you can pick investments, select a beneficiary, and determine how much money is invested. Some states will allow a state tax deduction.

The beneficiary is the future student. This student can be a child, grandchild, friend, or even yourself. The beneficiary must be a U.S. citizen or a resident alien with a valid social security number or taxpayer identification number. In the event that the beneficiary does not want to attend a higher education institution, there are several options. The investment can continue in the event that the beneficiary decides to attend school at a later time, or the owner can change the beneficiary to an eligible family member of the original beneficiary. There is no age limit for using the invested money. The invested money can be used to pay for anything that is considered a qualified higher education expense. Examples may include: tuition, books, room and board, computer hardware and software, internet services and related services, and required supplies.

The 529 account is not limited to college. The investment can pay for postsecondary trade and vocational schools, two-year and four-year colleges, and postgraduate programs. It does not matter where the student attends college. The student is not required to attend in their state of residence.

On our website, www.CollegeSurvivorBook.com, we provide a link to my personal financial advisor. I trust this firm. Their philosophy and mission statement are of high integrity. If you do not have a financial advisor and do not know where to start, they welcome your call.

The Smiths vs. the Jones
Let's compare two families:
$25,000 example (529 Planning)

The Smith Family

The Smith family invests $106 per month for 15 years for their one child under the age of three. After 15 years, the Smith family will invest $19,000 for their child's future education. The $19,000 investment will grow to $25,000 (6% return on investment).

The Jones Family

The Jones family does not invest for their one child under the age of three. Sure enough, they now have a very bright and talented college-bound child. Mr. and Mrs. Jones have no choice but to borrow. Now, they are faced with borrowing $25,000 at an annual interest rate of 8%. Unfortunately, the payments start after accruing interest during four years of college. The Jones family will pay $320 for 10 years, with interest of $13,000. Ultimately, the $25,000 that they borrowed will cost $38,000.

Now, Let's Add *College Survivor Strategy* to This Comparison and See What Happens.

It is high school graduation day for the Smith and Jones families. Both families have a college-bound child, but planned differently. In this case, the Smith family heard about *College Survivor Strategy* and started the process when their child was in kindergarten. The Smith family also heard about *College Survivor Strategy* but chose not to participate. Let's take a look at each bank account on high school graduation day.

The Smith Family Bank Account on High School Graduation Day

Amount	Action / Planning
$119,580.00	Parents embraced *College Survivor* strategy from Kindergarten to 12th Grade = $119,580*
$25,000.00	Parents invested in a 529 Savings since age 3: $106 per month / $3.48 per day or an investment of $19,000 with a return of $6,000 = $25,000**
$17,648.00	The Smith child worked full time during high school based on the *College Survivor* employment model and saved 70% for College = $17,648.00.***
$162,228.00	**The Smith child will graduate debt free before starting college.**

*Time and payout matrix, chapter 1, page 13 **The Smiths vs. The Jones, chapter 4, page 39 ***HS paycheck, 12 months, Chapter 15, page 128.*

On senior high school graduation day, the bank is filled with $162,228.00. The Smith student has not even started college and has an entire four years of college completely funded. The Smith child is prepared to graduate from college debt-free from day one.

Can the Smith Child Continue *College Survivor Strategy*? Yes!

If the Smith child continues to embrace *College Survivor Strategy* throughout their four years of college, despite the fact that their education is completely funded, the Smith student can expect to have a minimum of $80,000 in the bank on college graduation day. This will allow for studying abroad, attending graduate school, or postgraduate school. The only thing the Smith student must do is thank Mom and Dad for teaching them *College Survivor Strategy* and mentoring them how to save their money while working in high school.

What about the Jones student? It seems like the situation would be unbearable. Well, the Jones student comes from a normal modern-day family trying to make ends meet. Does the Jones student have a fat bank roll? There may be some savings, but not as much as the Smith student. And that is okay too! The Jones student can begin *College Survivor Strategy* and graduate debt free just like the Smith student.

The totals above are estimates. Students can win more money or less money. It all depends on the situation. As a parent, you will become a pro, and then teach your student, so they can become a pro. This is a great method in the case of a student that desires graduate school or a postgraduate school. When in graduate school and in pursuit of a doctorate, there is sometimes no time for work. Monies need to be standing by. There are scholarships for graduate school and for postgraduate school. Your student just needs to apply.

Is This Realistic?

"There is so much propaganda that indicates students win $500,000 to $1,000,000 in scholarships. I would say that for effort on a slow scale, this is certainly realistic. We have been using the strategy at our home, and it is working. Our family started late and learned a valuable lesson. Now, we are scrambling to catch up. The good news is, these are not hypotheticals. I have referred to the work hours that my own high school senior works on top of her academic and extra-curricular load as examples in this book, because they are in real time. Our family is looking at approximately ten to twelve years of a college learning curve with our two college-bound high school children. Both have hefty aspirations and we are a smart poor family, so we must have a plan. I am a mom who researches everything and asks a lot of questions. It is our hope that College Survivor Strategy will function as your one-stop shop of information and a teaching model for your children and grandchildren and **teach you the art of earning scholarships from kindergarten to grad school and beyond."**

P. Solis-Friederich, mom and author

Resources available at
www.CollegeSurvivorBook.com / University of Success section!
Remember! Believe in Yourself! You've Got This

"*I can remember a college friend talking about this thing called 'financial aid.' I had no idea what it was or how it worked. My parents borrowed money to send me to college my freshman year. Before the end of my first semester, my parents graciously informed me that they could no longer assist and that I would have to work. I can remember the look on my parents' face. They looked as if they had let me down. I could feel their despair. I maintained silence in respect for their pain. I had no idea what to do or how to do it.*"

P. Solis-Friederich, the college freshman

CHAPTER 5
FINANCIAL AID
USING YOUR FREE RESOURCES TO THE FULLEST

"It doesn't matter how many resources you have,
if you don't know how to use them,
it will never be enough."
--Anonymous

In This Chapter

1. The award letter

2. What is a scholarship?

3. What are student loans?

4. What is a work-study?

5. What are grants?

Know your basic resources and use them to their fullest. This is how knowledge becomes power! In this chapter, you will find a brief description of each topic. At the beginning of each section (except scholarship), you will find a link to https://studentaid.ed.gov/sa/. This is the most reliable site for in-depth information on each topic. There are numerous regulations and law changes that could affect the information. After reviewing the description in each section, it is advisable to check the website for application instructions, regulations, restrictions, and any changes. A link to this website is available on www.CollegeSurvivorBook.com.

The Award Letter

Dear parents and students,

Days before I sent in the manuscript of this book to my publisher, my child's college award letter showed up in the mail. The numbers were huge. I went into a panic mode, and the look on my child's face was that of fear. I could not believe my reaction! If I was responding this way, then all the other parents in this country must also be responding the same way, plan or no plan. We are all human! When I calculated the total financial debt for four years in college, my heart raced. I thought, how are we going to pay for this?

It was a reality check! Here I sat, with a completed book that provides answers to the problems of closing the financial gap with a step-by-step teaching guide. And I was panicked? I went back to my computer and used the calculators that I had spent endless hours designing for College Survivor Strategy. I entered the information in seconds, only to find that my child's job plus her scholarships provided a positive balance—relief and an affirmation that College Survivor Strategy works!

We are all human and initially react with emotion even if we have a solid plan. The calculators saved me that day. I had such relief. I did not have to pull out a personal calculator, paper, and pencil and try to figure this out. That would have taken hours, not to mention the mistakes and the stress. Thank goodness for the calculators. They are user-friendly and available on www.CollegeSurvivorBook.com *in the University of Success section.*

P. Solis-Friederich, the frantic mom

What Is a Scholarship?

A scholarship is a monetary award that does not require repayment. Surfing the internet will provide numerous scholarships. Another way of finding scholarships in a more organized fashion is by visiting a large bookstore and thumbing through the scholarship catalog books. These books will typically be 8" x 11" or larger and at least eight hundred pages long. You will be able to look by category and find scholarships you did not even know existed. This will be the best purchase for your college career.

Some examples of scholarship categories include academics, leadership, community service, humanities/arts, social sciences, sciences, state of residence, membership, ethnicity, race, family situations, sexual orientation, gender, disability, illness, companies, unions, organizations, etc.

Other places to look:

❖ Your local community organizations

❖ The magic drawer in your high school guidance counselor's office

❖ Your high school website and other high school websites

❖ Your college website and other college websites

❖ Student clubs

❖ Student organizations

What Is a Student Loan?

Source: https://studentaid.ed.gov/sa/

A loan is money that you borrow and must pay back with interest over a period of time. Although the interest rates are low, loans can add up very quickly and get out of control. Try to borrow the least amount of money possible if you are placed in a situation where you must take out a loan. Consider your career field and your potential salary and ability to pay back the loan. Federal loans are a much better option than private loans and credit cards. Borrow wisely. With *College Survivor Strategy*, loans should be the last option.

Questions to Ask Your College Financial Aid Advisor:

❖ Is this a federal student loan?

❖ Is this a private loan?

❖ What is the difference between the various loans that are offered?

❖ What is the interest rate?

❖ What are the repayment options?

❖ Are the repayment options flexible?

How Do I Get a Federal Student Loan?

To apply for a federal student loan, you must complete the FAFSA® (Free Application for Federal Student Aid). Your college or career school will send you a financial aid offer, which may or may not include federal student loans. Your school will tell you how to accept all or a part of the loan.

Where Do Loans Come from?

Loans can come from the federal government or private sources.

The William D. Ford Federal Direct Loan (Direct Loan) Program is the largest federal student loan program. Under this program, the U.S. Department of Education is your lender. Included are the following:

Direct Subsidized Loans

For undergraduate students who demonstrate financial need to help cover the costs of higher education at a college or career school. Undergraduates can borrow $5,500 to $12,500 per year depending on certain factors, including the year in college. Graduate students can borrow up to $20,500 per year.

Direct Unsubsidized Loans

Available to eligible undergraduate, graduate, and professional students, but in this case, the student does not have to demonstrate financial need to be eligible for the loan. Undergraduates can borrow $5,500 to $12,500 per year depending on certain factors, including the year in college.

Direct PLUS Loans

Available to eligible graduate or professional students and parents of dependent undergraduate students to help pay for education expenses not covered by other financial aid. Credit check is required for a parent loan (called PLUS loan).

Direct Consolidation Loans

Available for the purpose of allowing a combination all of your eligible federal student loans into a single loan with a single loan servicer.

The Federal Perkins Loan Program

A school-based loan program for undergraduates and graduate students with exceptional financial need. Under this program, the school is the lender. Undergraduates can borrow up to $5,500 per year and graduate students can borrow up to $8,000 per year, depending on financial need and with consideration of the amount of other aid you receive and the availability of funds at your college.

Keep in mind if you must take out a loan:

❖ The interest rate on federal student loans is almost always lower than private loans—and much lower than that on a credit card!

❖ You don't need a credit check or a cosigner to get most federal student loans.

❖ You do not have to begin repaying your federal student loans until after you leave college or drop below half-time.

❖ If you demonstrate financial need, you can qualify to have the government pay your interest while you are in school.

❖ Federal student loans offer flexible repayment plans and options to postpone your loan payments if you're having trouble making payments.

❖ If you work in certain jobs, you may be eligible to have a portion of your federal student loans forgiven if you meet certain conditions.

❖ Understand the legal obligation.

❖ Be a responsible borrower.

❖ Keep track of how much you're borrowing.

❖ Think about how the amount of your loan will affect your future finances and how much you can afford to repay. Your student loan payments should be only a small percentage of your salary after you graduate, so it is important to not borrow more than you need for your school-related expenses.

❖ Understand the terms of your loan and keep copies of your loan documents. When you sign your promissory note, you are agreeing to repay the loan according to the terms of the note even if you don't complete your education, can't get a job after you complete the program, or didn't like the education you received.

❖ Make payments on time. You are required to make payments on time even if you don't receive a bill, repayment notice, or a reminder. You must pay the full amount required by your repayment plan, as partial payments do not fulfill your obligation to repay your student loan on time.

❖ Keep in touch with your loan servicer. Notify your loan servicer when you graduate, withdraw from school, drop below half-time status, transfer to another school, or change your name, address, or social security number. You also should contact your servicer if you're having trouble making your scheduled loan payments. Your servicer has several options available to help you keep your loan in good standing.

What Is a Work-Study?

Source: https://studentaid.ed.gov/sa/

Federal Work-Study provides part-time jobs for undergraduate and graduate students with financial needs, allowing them to earn money to help pay education expenses. The program encourages community service work and work related to the student's course of study.

❖ It provides part-time employment while you are enrolled in school.

❖ It's available to undergraduate, graduate, and professional students with financial need.

❖ It's available to full-time or part-time students.

❖ It's administered by schools participating in the Federal Work-Study Program.

❖ Not all schools participate—ask your financial aid advisor.

Questions to ask your Financial Aid Advisor:

❖ Do you offer a work-study program?

❖ What kinds of jobs are there?

❖ Are jobs on campus or off campus?

❖ How much can I earn?

❖ How will I be paid?

❖ Can I work as many hours as I want?

❖ Are there restrictions?

❖ Are there jobs relevant to my course work?

Note: Your work-study award will depend on when you apply, your financial need, and your school's funding level. Most work-study programs pay minimum wage. Consider how your wage will affect your income and the impact on paying your college tuition and room and board. Consider the pros and cons of a minimum wage position if it is in your field of study.

What Is a Grant?

Source: https://studentaid.ed.gov/sa/

Grants are similar to scholarships. Grants are sometimes called "gift aid'. Grants are free money that does not require repayment. Most grants are need based, while scholarships are merit based. Grants are available from the federal government, state government, colleges and private or non-profit organizations.

Pell Grant

Federal Pell Grants are usually awarded only to undergraduate students. The amount of aid you can receive depends on your financial need, the cost of attendance at your school, and more. Federal Pell Grants are usually awarded only to undergraduate students who have not earned a bachelor's or a professional degree. (In some cases, however, a student enrolled in a post baccalaureate teacher certification program might receive a Federal Pell Grant.) A Federal Pell Grant, unlike a loan, does not have to be repaid, except under certain circumstances.

Effective July 1, 2012, you can receive the Federal Pell Grant for no more than twelve semesters or equivalent (roughly six years). You'll receive a notice if you're getting close to your limit. If you have any questions, contact your financial aid office. If you're eligible for a Federal Pell Grant, you'll receive the full amount you qualify for—each school participating in the program receives enough funds each year from the US Department of Education to pay the Federal Pell Grant amounts for all its eligible students. The amount of any other student aid for which you might qualify does not affect the amount of your Federal Pell Grant.

FSEOG Grant

A Federal Supplemental Educational Opportunity Grant (FSEOG) is a grant for undergraduate students with exceptional financial need. To get an FSEOG, you must fill out the free application for Federal Student Aid (FAFSA®) so your college can determine how much financial need you have.

Students who will receive Federal Pell Grants and have the most financial need will receive FSEOGs first. The FSEOG does not need to be repaid, except under certain circumstances. The FSEOG program is administered directly by the financial aid office at each participating school and is therefore called "campus-based" aid. Not all schools participate. Check with your school's financial aid office to find out if it offers the FSEOG.

Iraq and Afghanistan Grant

If your parent or guardian died as a result of military service in Iraq or Afghanistan, you may be eligible for an Iraq and Afghanistan Service Grant. Like other federal grants, Iraq and Afghanistan Service Grants provide money to college or career school students to help pay for their education expenses.

However, Iraq and Afghanistan Service Grants have special eligibility criteria. Learn how the automatic federal budget cuts, known as the "sequester," will affect the Iraq and Afghanistan Service Grant Program.

Military Family Information

Both the federal government and nonprofit organizations offer money for college to veterans, future military personnel, active duty personnel, or those related to veterans or active duty personnel.

What Financial Aid Does the Government Offer for Military Service or for Family Members of Military Personnel?

- ❖ Reserve Officers' Training Corps (ROTC) scholarships
- ❖ Department of Veterans Affairs (VA) education benefits
- ❖ Iraq and Afghanistan Service Grant or additional Federal Pell Grant funds

What is the TEACH Grant?

Source: https://studentaid.ed.gov/sa/

A Teacher Education Assistance for College and Higher Education (TEACH) Grant can help you pay for college if you plan to become a teacher in a high-need field in a low-income area. You'll be required to teach for a certain length of time, so make sure you understand your obligation. A TEACH Grant is different from other federal student grants because it requires you to take certain kinds of classes to receive the grant and do a certain kind of job to keep the grant from turning into a loan. The TEACH Grant program provides grants of up to $4,000 a year to students who are completing or plan to complete course work needed to begin a career in teaching.

NOTES

A list of preformatted questions is available in Chapter 17, page 181-183 and on www. CollegeSurvivorBook.com in the University of Success section.

My questions:

1.

2.

3.

4.

Resources available at
www.CollegeSurvivorBook.com / University of Success section!
Remember! Believe in Yourself! You've Got This!

51

The Story Behind Silly Rich and Smart Poor

"I have a family member who scraped by on pennies to raise her two daughters. She was a single parent. She could make a family meal on $3.00. She washed dishes at a restaurant for extra money. As she washed dishes, her baby sat in a baby carrier under the cash register. The baby was safe and with Mom, and there weren't any childcare costs. This is an example of total sacrifice to put food on the table. I became her student when I became a single parent in college. She showed me how to stretch every dollar. I learned how life is not about money and that you don't have to be rich to be happy. She was not rich, but she was wealthy. Without her teaching me how to find another way to make it in this world, I don't know if I would have had the skills. Smart poor is an art. She mastered the art, and then taught me."

P. Solis-Friederich, the smart poor college student

CHAPTER 6
SILLY RICH VS. SMART POOR
THE ART OF STRETCHING THE DOLLAR

> *"Don't buy things with money you don't have*
> *to impress people you don't like."*
> *--Dave Ramsey*

In This Chapter

Academic/College Related

1. Books & media, class fees, field of study

2. Extra-curricular

3. Fraternities and sororities

Personal/Living

1. Food and beverage

2. Transportation: around campus, traveling home

3. Shelter: first apartment selection, furnishings, summer, parents

4. Wardrobe, washing clothes

5. Cell phone, electronics, TV

6. Playtime/socializing/events

7. Medical, legal fees

8. Parent orientation

Tip: Have a Budget! It is best to create a budget for the extra-cost categories listed below. This way, you are not surprised with hidden costs and are not placed in a situation of funding a needed item without cash flow. Below are some hidden costs that need a budget. How you approach each cost determines if you are silly rich or smart poor.

Academic/College Related

Books and Media: $850 to $1,000

Silly rich student might buy new books rather than old books and spend closer to $1,000. Then, they may give their books away or trade them in for a fraction of the cost, such as $10 per book.

Smart poor student probably saves their gas, time, and energy and orders a used book online with a coupon code. They will most likely take care of their books because they plan on reselling them. They may buy a $125 book for $25 as a used book, then sell it for $45 to a friend or online. Just because they bought a $125 book for $25 online doesn't mean that they can't sell it for any amount they choose. There is a buyer for every product in this world. This person takes the profit and reinvests it in books for the next semester. Investing once and reselling could eventually reduce their book costs to $500 per semester. Chances are, the smart poor student might have a savings account that accrues interest, and this is where they place their book money.

Class Fees (Examples: Art Class, Science Lab, and Chemistry)

Silly rich student pays full price.

Smart poor student has been working hard using *College Survivor Strategy* and earning scholarships and grants to pay the fees.

Suggestion: The best way to find out about fees is to ask students who have taken the same class. If you can't find out the information from friends, the most accurate and reliable source would be your academic advisor. They will know or send you to someone who does know. Unfortunately, there isn't a way to reduce these fees. The fees are policy-based and non-negotiable.

Major (Field of Study) Related Costs

Some issues that could arise may include certain majors requiring students to study abroad or travel internationally to satisfy requirements for internship or required worksites. No matter what your major is, ask if there are requirements for foreign travel or major specific trips. This will require investigation with your academic advisor and visiting with your department of study. Most universities will have an administrative assistant working for the dean of your field of study. It is a good idea to ask this administrative assistant this question.

Extra-Curricular Costs

Silly rich student may not weigh the pros and cons of potential costs and time requirements when choosing an activity.

Smart poor students are more methodical in their thinking. They will take a moment to weigh the pros and cons of potential costs. This student will decide if it is worth their time and if they will benefit in the long run. Smart poor students are great decision-makers and can see how decisions will impact their pocketbook.

Suggestion: Just like in high school, participating in organizations outside of the classroom comes with a price tag. Clubs, intramural sports, and memberships will most likely require the purchase of T-shirts or membership memorabilia, in addition to travel costs such as hotel, gas, and food. Weigh the pros and cons and find the right place for you that is affordable. Most importantly, be happy!

Fraternity and Sorority Costs

The Greek system is very expensive. Dues are usually required (from modest to expensive) and joining halfway through the year can require paying retroactively, which can double the dues. Expect additional required Greek spending, like clothing for special events and traveling. The Greek system can be an investment for a foot in the door to a career. Deciding if this social network is worth your college budget is your decision. Weigh the pros and cons. Keep in mind that there are requirements for attendance to events, so you will not have as many opportunities to use your smart poor techniques. This is your call.

Personal/Living

Food and Beverage

Silly rich student may sometimes eat out every day because it is convenient and quite tasty. But they may forget to use the BOGO coupons and pay the full price.

Smart poor student eats out based on a budget and uses coupons. They know how to take advantage of the dollar menu! This student will cook at home to save money.

Transportation: Around Campus

Silly rich student will most likely park on campus. The struggle is finding a spot close to class. Another problem might be parking in the wrong place by accident, which can result in a ticket. Ouch! More money! Every college and university has different prices. If this student must pay a hefty $400 (parking fee) per year for four years, the total is $1,200. In the north, snow is an issue. Shoveling takes time. Driving takes time, and the potential for collision increases. Add the cost of gas and wear and tear on the car, which reduces the resale value. This student may or may not have roadside assistance for emergencies.

Smart poor student carpools or takes the shuttle. The shuttle is less expensive and drops the student close to their destination. The shuttle also has special entrances and exits for ease of movement. What a luxury! This student can study as they sit in the shuttle. Time is limited, so they make the most of it. The added bonus is this student may meet new people and grow an invaluable network of contacts. The larger the network of friends, the more resources. This student may also have a bike or moped for warm weather and save the car for groceries and going out with friends. This student may or may not have roadside assistance for emergencies.

Transportation: Traveling Home

Silly rich student might have forgotten to budget for gas. If they need to fly, they might buy an airline ticket at the last minute. Very expensive.

Smart poor student has a budget for gas. If they need to fly, they buy their airline ticket with parents' frequent flier miles and fly free. If there are no frequent flier miles, they buy their airline ticket months in advance. A smart poor student receives weekly email specials from their airline of choice and takes advantage of the sale. If travel is not realistic, they Skype to stay in touch.

Shelter: The First Apartment. How Exciting!

Silly rich student will most likely pick their apartment based on emotion. This is confusing the difference between need and want. They may want the apartment because it is luxurious or really cool. This student probably has not done their homework to find out how expensive utilities may be or if there are extra expenses if it's a gated community. This student may or may not have pets. But if they do, they may or may not pay the pet fee. If pets are prohibited, this student might have a contraband pet and risk being evicted or paying a hefty fine. This student will most likely pay full price for Wi-Fi and Cable and either live alone or have only one roommate. As for bills, this student may or may not pay on time. If this student is a habitually late payer, they will pay late fees over and over and wreck their credit without knowing it.

Smart poor student takes their time to look at numerous options. This student will most likely pick their apartment based on need rather than want. This student has probably done their homework to find out how expensive utilities are. This student may or may not have pets. But if they do, they pay the pet fee to cover any loss the pet may have caused. If pets are prohibited, this student finds an alternative like a fish or an iguana. This student will look for an apartment that offers free Wi-Fi. This student probably has one or more roommates to reduce the price, and they have a plan B for when a roommate moves out. This student may or may not pay on time. More than likely, this student pays on time because they cannot afford the late fees.

Suggestion: Try to rent for six months or month-to-month if it is less expensive. Getting locked into a year and running into roommate problems will be very expensive. Be aware of first and last deposits. Make sure that you collect your last deposit when you move out. Ask about the requirements for cleaning before moving out and how much will be charged if the cleaning is not to the apartment complex's standards. Find out what the standards are. Get a list. Call the utility company to find out the average cost of electricity, water, and gas to determine whether you can afford the apartment. Look for an all-bills-paid apartment. You will save by not paying a deposit for utilities, and you will have fewer bills. Look for an apartment with free Wi-Fi and cable. If not available, be prepared to pay for monthly Wi-Fi, but have a roommate split the cost with you. Make a good decision about pets and the deposits; get a fish! Live with several roommates. This way, if one moves out, the monthly rent is not as devastating. If you have lived in the dorm and shared a room, you can do it again. It is only temporary. Pay bills on time to establish good credit and avoid late fees. And finally, live with your parents if you are going to community college. This will save you $12,000 per year.

Shelter: First Apartment Furnishings

Silly rich student may find new furniture with low payments that include interest. The new furniture would most likely end up costing three to four times the original price. This is another case of want vs. need and an emotional buy. Other students may rent furniture, but this still adds up. $25 per month for your favorite sofa just cost you $900 plus interest for 36 months, and you have to pay the delivery to and from the store. Plus, it is not even yours to keep and resell. Heading to the store to buy everything new for the kitchen, bedroom, living room, and bathroom, plus decorations, can cost thousands of dollars. After graduation, many students haul their college apartment stuff to a thrift store as a donation. Granted, a donation is an incredible gesture, but at this time in your life, money management is critical.

Smart poor student is the ultimate in frugal. This student will buy furniture, dishes, pots and pans, and everything else from Goodwill, Salvation Army, thrift stores, Craig's List, and social media swap groups. There is always a student graduating that needs to sell their stuff. Smart poor student takes advantage of this situation. Then, when this student graduates, they turn right back around and sell everything to the next student. What an entrepreneur!

You already have items from the dorm such as bedding, towels, lamps, decorations, a desk, laundry baskets, waste baskets, bulletin boards, hair dryers, and even storage and small appliances. You will need a new list of things that you're missing, like a vacuum, cleaning supplies, other electronics, and things to set up a kitchen, bathroom, and living room.

Shelter: Summer

Do not forget to budget for summer housing, and if you plan to study abroad, think about where you will store your items while you are gone. Sometimes you can sublet to a student or students while you are gone so you can come back to your apartment. Never leave your valuables in the apartment. Be sure that you run a background check on the person you are trusting with your living space. Evaluate the pros and cons of this decision. Is it risky? Are you renting to a friend or family member that you have known for years? It is not recommended to rent to strangers. Anything could happen. Have them sign a contract and pay for the entire summer upfront in the event that they leave unannounced. This includes friends and family. The other option is to place your items in storage or pay the rent for the summer yourself. It may be cheaper than starting over with first and last month deposits and utility deposits. Only you can make this decision.

Shelter: Parents; Thinking Outside the Box

If you are able, is it possible to buy a home or mobile home? This way, your student can live rent free and you can charge for renting out bedrooms. When your student graduates, continue to rent out to other students until you can sell your property. Weigh all options and consult your financial advisor. You could make a profit.

Wardrobe

Silly rich student could be an impulse buyer. They may not take advantage of sales and coupons for buying online.

Smart poor student buys the same thing at consignment stores for a fraction of the cost. Most items still have the tags, and they buy based on need rather than want. They also take advantage of off-season sales and find similar full-priced items online from discount online retailers.

Suggestion: Does back-to-school clothing shopping really have to be an annual affair? Is there something wrong with the old wardrobe?

Washing Clothes

Suggestion: You will spend more money using quarters for washing and drying than buying a used washer and dryer. At first, it may seem like a few quarters are not such a big thing, but then you will start to notice that every week you are spending $20 or more on washing and drying. This adds up very quickly. $20 over 52 weeks is $1,040 per year. If you plan to go to the laundromat for four years, the cost will be at least $4,160, plus gas and time. You can buy a used washer and dryer for maybe $300 to $500. This will allow you to study while washing and drying and not have to travel. This is a huge time-saver. Can you imagine needing to wash clothes and your car doesn't start, or it is raining or snowing?

Cell Phone

Silly rich student wants the latest phone because it is the latest phone. They also pay an outrageous bill every month.

Smart poor student uses the pay-per-month plan and buys a new cell phone when the old one stops working. When they are forced to buy a new phone, they buy last year's model and save money.

Electronics

Silly rich student will most likely buy everything new. They will want the latest and greatest. This could be a confusion of want versus need and an emotional buy.

Smart poor student will buy last year's model or shop online for discounted models with coupon codes. They will buy only if they need rather than want. Who doesn't want the latest model? We all do, but this student does not fall into the social pressure of the latest and greatest. They will wait until their electronics give out then buy.

TV

Suggestion: Watching TV is a good time to decompress. It does not have to be expensive. Ask if your new apartment offers cable. If not, share the cost with your roommate. And ask yourself if it is worth it. If you are rarely home, watch your favorite show at school. There are flat screens everywhere. You can also pay less by watching TV on your laptop with a cable to a flat screen that you bought for next to nothing on Craig's List.

Play Time/Socializing/Events

Silly rich student may buy regular-priced tickets to events even though there are ways to get discount tickets. This student may confuse want vs. need and want the front row tickets (most expensive) even if they do not need them. This student will most likely spend without regard to a budget and may not have a budget or know how to budget. This student may spend rent money to attend the "concert of the century" and not be aware of protecting the basics: food, shelter, and transportation. On the opening night of a blockbuster movie, this student is first in line and pays the full price.

Smart poor student finds discount tickets online and uses coupon codes. This student usually does not pay the full price for anything unless it is very, very important and they have saved for it. This student will typically buy the backrow tickets that are less expensive and still have a great time. They are aware of the basics—food, shelter, and transportation—and would most likely not spend their rent money on entertainment. This student has great discipline and self-control. As for the block-buster movie, this student will wait a week for it to hit the discount movie theatre or then go to the matinee.

Suggestion: Determine your budget, and then pick the entertainment that is most important and fits into your budget. Save for things that are expensive but important to you. Social life is important, but it does not have to be expensive. Waiting a week or two and going to the discount movie is a matter of discipline. Does it really matter if you go to the opening night? Is the opening night of a new movie any different than waiting two weeks later to see the same movie in a less crowded the-atre? If a student only goes to movies on discount nights, they can see multiple movies in one night. Planning and budgeting properly could allow a student to go to the movies every week and see all the movies! How fun!

Medical

Ask your financial advisor about the college medical program and compare it to your medical insurance. Weigh the pros and cons. Make sure the college does not automatically charge you for insurance if you already have insurance. Have a plan of action, because if a student becomes ill and the parents live far away, they will need to know what to do.

Legal Fees

This is certainly not on your radar, and why should it be? But things happen. Some issues that could arise may include landlord/tenant problems, identity theft, scams, traffic accidents and violations, criminal issues (drug or alcohol use), or guilt by association—IT HAPPENS!

Parent Orientation

Expect colleges to offer parent orientation at the same time as student orientation. These sessions are very important, as they are designed to educate parents on campus resources. A fee could be required. And expect to stay in a hotel if parents live far away. Parents should plan ahead. Hotels will be expensive because of supply and demand. Secure your hotel months in advance for a less expensive rate, or use your frequent flier miles. Also, ask if the university is offering a lodging program or a discount code at local hotels. Ask, and you shall receive. If you don't ask, how can you receive?

Ask Yourself

1. Are you silly rich or smart poor or a combination of both?

2. Which category provides the most struggles for you?

3. Which category would you like to see self - improvement?

4. What is your plan?

5. What is the start date of your plan?

6. Your Commitment Statement:

"When you are a single parent in college with pennies to stretch, you learn the difference between want and need overnight."

P. Solis-Friederich, the dollar-stretching college student

CHAPTER 7
NEED VS. WANT
WHO IS IN CONTROL? YOU OR YOUR EMOTIONS?

> *"It is not an issue of wants vs. needs.*
> *It's an issue of wants vs. priorities."*
> *--Anonymous*

In This Chapter

1. Want vs. need

2. Food

3. Shelter

4. Transportation

WANT Is Emotional. Need Is a PRIORITY!

When living at home with your family, can you remember saying things like "I want a new iPhone" or "I need new clothes?" Depending on your situation, either these items were provided or, in some cases, you funded the needs and wants. College is practice for adulthood. This is why you may feel overwhelmed and stressed. You are placed in a situation where you have to make the decisions and you have to learn from them.

The basic needs are food, shelter, and transportation. That is it. Everything else is want. Money must fund these basic needs. Many students fund these needs through loans. This astounds me. Whether you are in school or not, you still need food, shelter, and transportation. So, if you are not in school, would you take out a loan for these basic needs? Would your family take out a loan for these basic needs? No!

How you make decisions is based on how you were raised. You watched the actions of those who raised you. Just like snowflakes, all situations are unique and different. Let's take a look at some situations.

I want a new car:

Could you save money and buy a used car?

Does your current car get you from point A to point B?

Why do you need a new car?

What is your MPG?

I want a new phone:

Does your current phone still work?

Do you need to spend $800+ on a new phone?

Will this cause you to fall short on rent?

Can you find a less expensive way?

Could you request this phone as a Christmas present?

I want a new tattoo, but it is expensive:

Can you save each week for this luxury?

Will this impact your money flow for food, shelter, and transportation?

I want new clothes:

The new outfit is gorgeous, but it costs $80. Clothes can help the self-esteem.

Can you use coupons to pay for this?

Can you visit consignment stores and find the same thing with tags and pay a few dollars?

Can you find the same or similar online for $10?

Also, do you have plenty of clothes and is it necessary?

Salesmen Know Your WANT!

When you are shopping and engage with a salesperson, they have been trained to ask you questions and find your want. An amazing salesperson will convince you that you need what you want. You will be convinced that you need a product when you only want the product. Manipulation of emotions is how this happens. How do I know this? Well, for seven years in my corporate career, I trained adult salespeople how to sell.

Has it happened to me? Of course! Recently, I made the mistake of visiting the cosmetic counter in a department store. I needed foundation makeup. The salesperson determined my want and manipulated my emotions into a need. Before it was all over, I had bought toner, wrinkle cream, eye cream, day cream, night cream, makeup remover, and more. I only needed foundation and was prepared to pay $40. I walked out with $250 charged to my credit card. Boy, I looked great. I looked younger and less tired, and my self-esteem improved. I let my emotions make the decision. We are all human!

Your basic NEEDS are Food, Shelter and Transportation.

FOOD

Remember! Eat to live rather than live to eat!

Ask Yourself:

Do I pay full price for food?

Do I use coupons?

Do I use the weekly ad?

Do I buy the full price value meal or use the dollar menu at fast food?

Am I a habitual fast food addict?

What are my habits?

How can I improve?

SHELTER

Remember, you need shelter. It does not have to be expensive or luxurious. This is college. Stretch that dollar! When you graduate debt free, you will be able to buy your dream house and live the life you want!

Ask Yourself:

Can I find a less expensive place to live?

Can I add a roommate or two?

Can I reduce this cost?

What is my current situation? Can I change it?

TRANSPORTATION

Ask Yourself

Is my vehicle safe?

Do I have good gas mileage?

Is my vehicle constantly in the shop and costing me unnecessary money?

Do I take advantage of the school shuttle? Is a moped a better solution?

Is my insurance too expensive?

What are my problems, and how can I fix them?

Let's look at the differences in three cars and how it may impact your budget. Ask yourself if you need to sell your car and find a better option. This is a good way to save money. Go to www.CollegeSurvivorBook.com in the University of Success section and you will find a link to learning more about MPG. If you are shopping for a new car and are looking at several options, you will be able to compare the options and weigh the pros and cons.

Vehicle Comparison - MPG

Car	*MPG	Miles driven per year	Price of gas	Gallons needed	Cost for 1 year	Cost for 4 years
#1	11	15,000	$ 2.40	1364	$ 3,272.73	$13,090.91
#2	21	15,000	$ 2.40	714	$ 1,714.29	$ 6,857.14
#3	32	15,000	$ 2.40	469	$ 1,125.00	$ 4,500.00

*MPG = Miles Per. Gallon

MPG Formula

Obtain the miles traveled from the trip odometer, or subtract the original odometer reading from the new one. Divide the miles traveled by the amount of gallons it took to refill the tank. The result will be your car's average miles per gallon yield for that driving period.

Gas Cost Formula

Miles Driven per year divided by MPG = gallons needed, then Price of Gas x Gallons Needed x 4 = Cost for 4 years. Example: (Car #1) 15,000 / 11 = 1364 then, $2.40 x 1364 = $3272.73 (for one year) x 4 (for four years) = $13,090.91

Savings

Buy a car with better gas mileage (Car #3) vs. (Car #1) and you will save $2,147.72 in one year and $8,590.91 in four years.

Resources available at
www.CollegeSurvivorBook.com / University of Success section!
Remember! Believe in Yourself! You've Got This!

67

Mrs. P. Friederich #1   *Mrs. P. Friederich #2*

Miss M. Friederich #3

"Our children are blessed to have two sets of grandparents that can provide invaluable advice for their future."

P. Solis–Friederich, learning and teaching parent

CHAPTER 8
THE GENERATION GAP
WHY DON'T I UNDERSTAND WHAT MY CHILD IS SAYING?

"The Future promise of any nation can be directly measured by the present prospects of its youth."
--John F. Kennedy

In This Chapter

1. The generations

2. Communication

3. Pros & cons of IGEN/Gen Z

4. Statistics of IGEN/Gen Z

5. Preparing for Gen alpha/linksters

6. Parents/grandparents

7. How older generations think

The Generations

The Student (as of 2018)

- IGEN/Gen Z (born 1995 to 2012), age 6 to 23
- Gen Alpha/Linksters (born 2013 to 2025), age <5

The Parent and Grandparents (as of 2018)

- Parents, grandparents, students born 1980 to 1994 (millennials)
- Parents, grandparents, students born 1975 to 1985 (xennials)
- Parents, grandparents, students born 1965 to 1979 (Gen X)

- Parents, grandparents, students born 1946 to 1964 (boomers)
- Grandparents born 1925 to 1945 (silent generation)

Communication

The purpose of this chapter is to assist with communication issues that arise from the generation gap.

If you cannot communicate with your child, then how can you help them with their transition to college? They cannot transition (successfully) alone. After evaluating several studies that agreed and disagreed on the definition of each and every generation, listed are the most accurate findings. This generation gap is cyclical, and there is no way of breaking the cycle. The only solution is understanding the generation gap differences and employing communication skills based on knowledge.

Pros and Cons of the IGEN/Gen Z

Below is a statistical analysis of the IGen/Gen Z generation. Hopefully, this will help parents and grandparents understand how this generation thinks and makes decisions.

As with any generation gap, communication is the biggest hurdle. Understanding the generation will help as you mentor your student. When you read the pros and cons, take into account that you are communicating with a different perspective on life. This is no easy task. If you can remember, when you were a teenager growing up in your generation, your parents were frustrated with why and how you made decisions. It is a constant cycle.

Pros of IGEN/Gen Z Generation

❖ Tolerant of others' culture, race, and sexual orientation. They know no different and really do not care.

❖ Not big risk-takers. They are very cautious.

❖ Less drinking and drug taking—I am not kidding. Statistics back this up!

❖ Less likely to go church and more likely to think for themselves.

❖ Most likely to not believe in authority in church or government.

❖ Less time in shopping malls.

❖ Less time going to the movies and would rather rent at home.

❖ More likely to use Instagram than Facebook.

Cons of IGEN/GenZ Generation

❖ Less likely to commit to a relationship.

❖ Face-to-face communication issues because of smartphones.

❖ Heavy gaming use.

❖ Does not read printed books or newspapers.

❖ Grew up more supervised than previous generations.

❖ Limited experience with teen jobs and earning money in high school.

❖ Potential for staying up past midnight on smartphone and social media.

❖ Potential for higher depression rate than prior generations.

❖ May feel lonely and not needed.

❖ Potential for a higher suicide rate.

Supervision

Parents, you have amazing children. They are in a generation that will lead the nation. The problem is that this generation continues to be ill-equipped to "grow up" because they have been over-protected and over-supervised (based on statistics). Despite the over-management, this generation has a strong mind and is very independent. A solution may be to allow this student to fail. Studies indicate that this generation is not allowed to fail, which leads to a lack of coping skills. Let them fall and allow them to find solutions to get themselves right back up.

High School Employment

As these students enter high school years, studies indicate that there is not enough employment practice to assist in the transition from high school to college. Despite the level of high school employment practice, college is and always will be a very big adjustment for any student. Keep in mind that employment builds confidence and social coping skills. High school employment is practice for adulthood and assists with a smoother transition to college and adulthood. The greatest gift that you can give to your high school student is to ensure that they work while in high school. No matter how busy they are, no matter what grades they have, encourage, encourage, encourage. This generation has been sheltered from this skill. You are the driving force behind changing this over-management issue.

Students benefit from learning work ethics, balancing academics and extra-curricular activities with a work schedule, and financial responsibility. The sooner they can begin paying for their own monthly cell phone bill, the better. You will be training them to transition to college. The ramifications of not allowing your student to work and taking on small financial responsibilities will create a rougher transition to college and adulthood. Studies indicate that a college student's greatest struggle is due to lack of skills.

Verbal Communication Skills on the Decline

Because of smartphones and the more reliant use of technology, this generation struggles with verbal communication. It only makes sense that this generation is less likely to commit to a relationship as quickly as other generations (statistically-based). Communication is one of the major ingredients in a personal relationship. Eliminate or reduce this critical ingredient (verbal communication and inter-action), and it is no wonder that this generation will not commit to a relationship. Most spend their time communicating via text rather than engaging in actual face-to-face verbal communication.

College Survivor and IGEN/Gen Z

College Survivor Strategy is predominantly designed for this generation. Since this generation does not read print books, they can buy the e-version and read on their phones or tablets, then go straight to our website. The videos on *College Survivor* University directly correlate with the chapters in the book. *College Survivor Strategy* serves this generation as a guide for work schedules, budgets, academic balance, life skills, and more. *College Survivor Strategy* is the core of the book, and designed to speak to parents, grandparents and students.

Preparing for Gen Alpha/Linksters
(born 2013 to 2025): Age <5

This generation is just in its infancy. Experts state that this generation could be a continuation of the prior generation. It is unknown whether this this future generation will have much of a change from the prior generation. We can expect more technology and continuation of problems with verbal communication. This generation may never even read a print book. As it is, physical bookstores are on the decline because of information available on the internet. Time will tell…

Parents/Grandparents

So, why bother to include grandparents in this section? Well, I just happen to have a savvy mother and mother in-law that were both born in 1933 and want to help their grandchildren with scholarships. Both are in their mid-80s yet well-versed on the internet! Also, not every child is raised by a parent. Many are raised by grandparents, foster homes, or with other family and friends. There are so many situations today's child can be placed in.

The information in this chapter may not describe you, but it is based on statistics and is an overall example of each generation's population. As you can see, the generation gap continues, and so does the struggle with communication over core values, finances, education, and life balance.

Knowing and understanding how your generation sees the world might help in communication with the current and future generations.

How Older Generations Think

Birth Year	Name	Values	Finances	Education	Life Balance
1977 to 1994	Millennials / GenY / Gen Next	Individuality	Earn Now / Spend Now	Expensive	Work, Life, Community
1975 to 1985	Xennials	Cross-over generation - more like Gen X than Millennial	Cross-over generation - more like Gen X than Millennial	Cross-over generation - more like Gen X than Millennial	Cross-over generation - more like Gen X than Millennial
1965 to 1979	Gen X/Baby Bust	Time	Save	A path	Work, Family
1946 to 1964	Baby Boomers	Success	Buy Now / Pay Later	A birthright	Workaholics: imbalance work / family
1925 to 1945	Silent Generation	Family	Save	A dream	Work hard

Resources available at
www.CollegeSurvivorBook.com / University of Success section!
Remember! Believe in Yourself! You've Got This!

"My greatest coach, mentor, and #1 fan is still my Dad. He has been parenting me for over five decades, and he is still right."

P. Friederich, the daughter

CHAPTER 9
THE FIRST MENTOR IS THE PARENT
FIRST, YOU PUT ON YOUR SOCKS...

> *"A good coach can change a game,*
> *a great coach can change a life."*
> *--John Wooden*

In This Chapter

1. Expectations for your children

2. Let them Fall

3. Coaching the coach

4. True story of parent coaching

5. Coaching practice

6. Parent letter

This chapter is written for parents, grandparents, mentors, and any person assisting a child with the transition to college and adulthood.

For a teenager, these are tough minutes, days, weeks, and months. Adolescence is still adolescence. Being a teenager and having your body go berserk is no easy task. This metabolic change happens in every generation. Peer pressure still exists, and now there is cyber bullying. Adolescence has not changed one bit. The only thing that has changed is the environment and technology. These kids are going through the same changes that we all have.

The best way to be a coach is to find inspiration in something or someone great and passing it along. Before we start, this inspirational message is for you. Consider the little things and how important they are, as suggested by the famous John Wooden.

"Born on October 14, 1910, in Indiana, John Wooden became an all-American guard at Purdue University. After stints as a high school coach and teacher, he took over as head basketball coach at UCLA in 1948 and led the Bruins to a record 10 national championships. The first person to be inducted to the Basketball Hall of Fame as a player and coach, Wooden died in Los Angeles on June 4, 2010."

source: https://www.biography.com/people/john-wooden-21369183

John Wooden: First, How to put on your socks

"I think it's the little things that really count. The first thing I would show our players at our first meeting was how to take a little extra time putting on their shoes and socks properly. The most important part of your equipment is your shoes and socks. You play on a hard floor. So, you must have shoes that fit right. And you must not permit your socks to have wrinkles around the little toe—where you generally get blisters—or around the heels.

It took just a few minutes, but I did show my players how I wanted them to do it. Hold up the sock, work it around the little toe area and the heel area so that there are no wrinkles. Smooth it out good. Then hold the sock up while you put the shoe on. And the shoe must be spread apart—not just pulled on the top laces. You tighten it up snuggly by each eyelet. Then you tie it. And then you double-tie it so it won't come undone—because I don't want shoes coming untied during practice, or during the game. I don't want that to happen.

I'm sure that once I started teaching that many years ago, it did cut down on blisters. It definitely helped. But that's just a little detail that coaches must take advantage of, because it's the little details that make the big things come about."

source:http://www.newsweek.com/john-wooden-first-how-put-your-socks-167942

Expectations for Your Children

Considering no child is alike, your child may want to go to a trade school or not even want a higher education. You may have a child with special needs. No matter the situation, it is up to you to encourage and coach. Please know that they are watching you. You are the foundation of their future. How you act and what you say are considered "normal." Your children do not know any other way. Do not be fooled into thinking you have eighteen years to develop your child. You have six years—seventy-two months—for the first phase. Then you have another six years until they reach age twelve, or whenever the hormones knock on the door and steal your precious baby. Treasure each moment. Take pictures, write those moments in the baby book, and enjoy. Do not place yourself in a situation of regret such as, "Why did I miss the choir presentation or the baseball game?" Trust me; your child is more interested in seeing you in the audience than in the actual performance or event.

Let Them Fall

It is okay to protect and love your child, but it is also okay to let them fall and have them learn how to get up by themselves. College could be an overwhelming struggle not because of intellect, but because of lack of skills. Think back to how you learned.

Allow your child to make bad decisions.

I know my father left the door of bad decisions wide open so I could walk through, fall, get back up, and walk back through the door a changed person.

Our family is raising two children in this generation. As a parent, I learn from my children every day. And I do my best to keep that door of bad decisions open for them as well.

Belonging to generation X and having gone down the road five decades, I don't have a problem with my children falling and learning. So far, so good. And of course, lest we forget, my children are smarter than me. But one day, they will come back and find that I am wiser than they are. That day will come, just as I was smarter than my parents when I was a teenager, and just as most adult children run right back to the parent for advice! Have patience. For now, the greatest teachers of this generation are my children for the future and my parents for the past. I learn both ways. My research has helped me communicate with my children on their level. What a find!

Coaching the Coach

Now let's talk about college, your child, and your role. First, their career choice is theirs, not yours. They have their own passions and dreams. It is your job to coach them regarding how to turn those passions into goals. Remember, they do not have adult learning skills. At this time, you are their only mentor. Later in life, they will have other mentors, such as teachers, supervisors, religious leaders, friends, and sometimes strangers whom they meet for a split second, and yet may provide a compelling, life-changing thought. Turning their passions into goals can be one of the hardest things. They need guidance.

How many times have you heard someone say, "I don't know what I am going to do with my life?" The reason a person might say this is because they are not recognizing their passions. Until your child realizes their passion, goal setting is almost impossible. You are the coach! Parents, your child will benefit from any type of higher education, such as trade school, community college, certification to become a nurse aid, certification to become a mechanic, or beauty college, and the list goes on. There are scholarships for all these options! There is money to claim. It is important to read *College Survivor Strategy* to find out where these resources are located and, most importantly, how to develop and execute a plan.

Children, just like adults, have a passion that needs to be cemented into a goal. You can help them with encouragement and as a mentor. If you (the parent/mentor) must drive to the largest retail bookstore and look for books with a list of scholarships, then do it. Consider it a gift. You can also surf the web with the right keywords to find scholarships for your child. And do not forget that there are financial aids and grants waiting to be claimed. Help your child so they can help themselves. Remember, our parenting duties do not stop on the eighteenth birthday. And most parents want to see their child succeed in life.

True Story of Parental Coaching

Once, we were checking out at a large grocery store where we ran into a family (friends of my daughter). The oldest in the family had recently graduated from high school and was paying thousands of dollars for beauty school. She was working endless hours to pay for this school. She told me that she had dreams of having her own chain of salons. Wow! What a kid! She stated that the beauty college did not accept any financial aid and that she had no choice but to pay. I lifted her spirits by letting her know that there are endless scholarships for trade/specialty schools and that, in many cases, the foundation will send the check directly to the student. She couldn't believe it.

Standing next to her was her sister, a senior in high school. I asked her what her plans were. She stated that she wanted to be a writer or publisher, but money was an issue. I assured her that doors are not closed and that she could most certainly go to school and graduate as debt-free as possible. She replied with tears, "Really? I can go to college? I am so happy!" Their mother was not far away and only spoke Spanish. The girls told the news to their mother. I could see her relief through her smile, and she glowed. The mom blessed me and told me "thank you" in Spanish. It was a joy!

So, why is this a parent coaching story? Because the parents of these two girls wanted only the best for their children and supported their dreams and aspirations. Despite the language barrier, it was evident that these two girls had been coached, inspired, and mentored in their homes. After substitute-teaching and chatting with hundreds of students, I can say for certain that it is crystal clear when a student has been coached/mentored from home. It is also clear when they have not been coached/mentored from home, and that is a very sad day.

Dear Parent,

I write this section as a parent talking to another parent. I am not a licensed psychologist, nor do I have a formal degree in psychology. My degree is from the school of hard knocks of parenting. This is a world-wide university that everyone attends whether they like it or not. There are no scholarships for this school, but the education is priceless. I have three children, and each one is completely different. I have been a parent for thirty-two years. I see the potential in each child a different way. And I am proud of their accomplishments, as each one is so incredibly unique. It astounds me how each one can be so different even though they have the same house and the same parents. I am sure many of you reading this can relate.

Before my two youngest children were born, I watched a very dear friend struggle with one of her children. College was not for her child. This was so hard for her to accept, because she was raised with the idea that a higher education was considered the next step and not an option (just like me). Her middle child attempted college, only to find that it was not the best option. As a parent, she had to dig deep and support this child, and only offer words of inspiration for other options. Eventually, this child became an adult and had to make their own decisions. All she could do was watch, let them learn, fail, and succeed on their own terms. This is a very hard thing for a parent to do. She admitted, saying "I told you so" is not the best way to mentor your child. Instead, saying "I love you" and turning the situation around, putting the ball in their court, creates ownership. Saying positive things such as, "I have faith in you" or "I am proud of you, no matter what" or "So, what did we learn from this and what is your next plan?" prove to be more effective. I listened. I watched. I learned.

I have a story for you that happened later in my life. In this case, I was an observer but was also a student learning from another parent. I have a very close friend that has been parenting (and now grand-parenting) for over forty years. She had four children that led lives in four completely different ways. Her family endured several tragedies as some families do. Her advice to me was to love your children no matter what, and that we cannot control their decisions. Her mantra was, "It doesn't matter what they do. As a mother, my goal is for my children to be happy."

So, her formula was unconditional love without judgment. I did not understand this for the longest time, until my dearest friend was placed in similar shoes. With her oldest child, the only thing she could do was offer love unconditionally and pray that this child would find happiness. Her role model days were long past. All we can do as parents is plant the seed, water it, provide sunlight, and let it grow despite the weather. We cannot control the weather.

When I was a Girl Scout leader, I was asked to deliver a presentation to a room of fifty parents of new little Girl Scouts. Parents were attending because their "wife said so," or they "weren't sure," or "out of curiosity." They were parents from all walks of life, values, education levels, and financial levels. My goal was to create an even playing field and speak to the core. Take away the education, the money, and the judgment, and they were all parents. I spoke about how time flies, and that they have one chance to get this right. There are no do-overs, and no delete button with the option to rewrite history. I explained that all children are different, and to just love and encourage as best as you can. I showed them a model of the years of growth. Up to age five, they are completely dependent on the parent. The parent is the love of their life. They are watching their parents' actions and listening to the parents' words. This is what they will consider normal.

At age six to twelve, they will still be watching their parents and learning from the parents' words and actions, but they will start to socialize at school and find out that other homes are different than theirs. Starting around age twelve, the hormones will take over, and so many things will begin to happen that a parent will not understand. Parents will have to be prepared for frustration. I spoke about communication and how children will act differently and talk differently because of the cyclical generation gap. There is no escaping the generation gap.

Then, I explained about how at age thirteen, the parent, who was the child's only love in their life until then, could be replaced with a new "puppy love," and that there is no preparation for this transition. Then, from age fourteen to eighteen, this child would begin testing the waters, "because they can" and because they would be trying to find their purpose in life (Just as we did when we were growing up). Personally, there is not enough money in the world to pay me to go through adolescence a second time!

At the end of the presentation, I asked each parent to take the piece of paper I had placed on each table and write one word that would describe their commitment to their child—one single word that they could focus on. I asked them to fold this tiny piece of paper so that it could remain private. Then I asked them to place it in their wallet or in a place that only they see frequently. My purpose was to keep the parents focused on the task. Time was ticking, and six years goes by in a snap. In fact, eighteen years goes by in a snap. As a parent, you get one chance to make an impact on your child's life. Focus. Stay the course and follow your heart.

Parenting is the hardest job in the world. It is not like going to your paying job with tasks to achieve each day and deadlines. A paying job can be a constant evolution with tremendous change, or it can be "same stuff, different day." The good thing is you can go home and leave work at work.

Parenting is 24/7/365 for the rest of your life. My parents have been parenting me for fifty-one years. That is a long time to parent.

One of my children would ask, "Why do you still act like you are their child when they tell you what to do? You are an adult."

My answer is, "Because I am, and always will be, their child, and they deserve respect. Just because I am an adult of five decades does not mean I cannot continue to learn from my parents. They still have good advice, and I listen and learn. They have always supported me and continue to love me without condition. That is why!"

And you know, someday they will be gone. They are in their eighties. A parent's love is unbreakable.

Every time I take my family to visit my parents in Texas and we walk right through that same door from my childhood, the same sparkle and glow lights up the house. Their child is home, and love fills the air. My parents are still in mentoring mode. They are teaching me how to greet my children and grandchildren when I am in my geriatric years. We never stop learning from the actions of parents.

P. Solis-Friederich, the daughter and mother

"There is no such thing as a Perfect Parent.
So just be a Real One"
– Sue Atkins

COMMITMENT

On a small piece of paper write one word that describes your commitment to your college-bound child. Date it. Place it in a private spot. Commit.

SELF EVALUATION

Write your thoughts here or in a private place. Forget the past. Look to the future.

Resources available at
www.CollegeSurvivorBook.com / University of Success section!
Remember! Believe in Yourself! You've Got This!

"THE NEXT STEP. I was more than ready for college. I was so excited. Mom made sure I was "over packed." She thought of everything! After settling in, when my parents were ready to leave, my dad asked if I needed help to find the band hall for Flag Corp practice. I said no. I wish I had said yes. I saw a tear and a broken heart as he drove away with my mom and siblings."

P. Friederich, the college freshman daughter

CHAPTER 10
COUNTDOWN TO COLLEGE
48 MONTHS AND COUNTING

> *"Failing to plan is
> planning to fail."*
> --Alan Lakein

In This Chapter

1. *College Survivor:* planning tips

2. *College Survivor Strategy* (scholarships)

   a. Freshman to senior

3. High school student focus (academics and everything else)

   a. Freshman to senior

4. Calendar college prep checklist by month/year

   a. Freshman/sophomore years

   b. Junior year

   c. Senior year

This chapter annotates exactly what our family has endured over the past four years in preparation for our daughter to enter college. This encouragement is from one parent to another, and all situations are different. Here is the best advice from our situation, confirmed with research from all geographic areas in this country. These tips are for the hardworking family in America.

College Survivor Strategy: Planning Tips

Parents, eighteen years is a flash of time. If you can get ahead of the curve, you are a rock star! Play your cards right, and when college nears, you should have a full bank account, less stress, and the greatest gift to your child. The sooner you can start implementing *College Survivor Strategy*, the better!

Dream Team of Parents

Meet as per your calendar of commitment, like a scrapbooking club or guys'/girls' night out. Get creative and make it fun. After you have gone to the bookstore and found a college scholarship listing catalog that suits your family, you will be amazed at how many scholarships and contests there are, starting at kindergarten. Someone has to win these contests. It might as well be your child.

Smart Poor Rather Than Silly Rich

Anything can happen during the course of your child's life. Value the dollar, because it could be gone someday. Trust me; I know. Been there, done that. And when your child learns from your practices of being Smart Poor, they will already have the skills to cut costs in college.

Save

Save via the 529 plan or even a savings account at your bank; the investment is astounding. Remember: out of sight, out of mind. If you have this money taken straight out of your weekly or monthly paycheck, you will never know it was there or that it existed. It is never too late to start saving!

Countdown to College – 48 months

College Survivor Strategy: High School Freshman to Senior

Freshman and Sophomore Years

During these years, the best Dream Team method is for parents to organize and have your student assist. You are the mentor. Having a team of adults and students from different families will lessen the hormonal meltdowns because the setting is not private for the adolescent.

You might have less rolling of the eyes if the other parents have their children along. Don't be surprised if it turns into a competition. Peer pressure can assist the situation. Consider this conversation: "I applied for two scholarships!" vs. "Well, I just finished applying for my third scholarship."

And parents can be competitive too! It's interesting how an organization of minds can turn into a competition where everyone wins, but quite daunting as well. Family A may win $3,000 for their child, while family B wins $2500 for their child. Think! If these families had not been meeting as a Dream Team in the first place, both families would have $0, and their children would be less financially prepared for College.

Junior Year

The countdown has begun—twenty-four months to graduation! This is the make-or-break year. The majority of scholarships are due this year. Do not be fooled into thinking you can wait until the senior year. If you do, you have given up the chance for over 50% of the scholarships. That means someone else claimed your child's money. And the monies available during the junior year are huge! This is not the year to slack on Dream Team meetings. Money is on the table. Expect this to be a challenging year. Your student is more involved, classes are harder, they are working more, and they will take the PSAT—all in preparation for college. It is a good thing. It is okay. They won't melt, I promise!

Summer After Junior Year

This is when your student will write numerous essays for scholarship applications and prepare to take the SAT or ACT. There are summer classes, books, and online classes that will help them prepare. There will also be college visits and the beginning stages of making a career and college decision. Your child does not have academic responsibility in the summer. They are only working and socializing, so making the most of the summer is critical. Your senior year Dream Team planning schedule should be ready to go before the start of the year. Apply for scholarships early! The senior year is a rollercoaster! Even with this much activity, transitioning to college is still more stressful. The key is learning *College Survivor Strategy* skills, working, and managing time and stress at a very early age.

Senior Year

Snap, and it is over. There is so much to do the senior year: academics, extra-curricular activities, working, performances, competitions, attending online college courses at school, taking the SAT or ACT several times, etc. If you were able to master your strategy in your junior year, you should have money in the bank for your child and have momentum. This is a very stressful and exciting year, involving extra banquets, parties, expos, presentations, competitions, and so on.

High School Student Focus: High School Freshman to Senior

In the blink of an eye, your child is in high school. You thought you were busy in elementary school and middle school, but now, get ready to run. Below is a list of focus items for all four years in high school. If your child has been taking accelerated classes since middle school and is on the highway to taking college classes while in high school, you will need to work very closely with the school guidance counselor. Your child may or may not have decided on a career. And it is okay to have a change of mind. If your child has an older sibling who is visiting colleges or attending college, it is always a good idea to take your younger child along. This will create excitement and curiosity.

College-prep Courses

This will be impressive when your child applies for college, and you will save a lot of money.

Grades

Better grades provide better opportunities.

Extra-curricular and Leadership Activities

Colleges like to see a well-rounded candidate, and it is good for your child's self-esteem and social skill development.

Summer Volunteer Opportunities/Jobs/Internships

These are great for deciding on a major, gaining skills, building the resume, and earning some extra money.

High School Guidance Counselor

Always have this person on your child's side. They will think of your child when scholarships land on their desk.

Parents/Guardians

Talk early and be realistic with goal-setting. *College Survivor Strategy* can help you plan.

Student Resume

Start as soon as possible. Your job is to gather information for several years and organize at the end of your child's junior year. Find a safe place to write down their accomplishments after they happen, or you will forget. Perhaps use a notebook or a paper on the refrigerator. Keep a copy of all the programs that they are in, for reference. Store them in a storage bin. Just toss a copy in after a performance or an activity. You will be amazed at how many things your child can accomplish and how easy it is to forget. The most important thing is that you keep track of your child's academic milestones, volunteer experiences, clubs, elected positions, all extra-curricular events, competitions, newspaper articles etc.

The best time to document information is June 1st so that you may document the academic year. August 1st is also a good time to document summer milestones such as volunteering, traveling abroad, and receiving summer program awards. Place June 1st and August 1st on your calendar. Commit to documenting. It is very difficult to attempt to document four years of high school in one sitting.

Student Banking and Savings

Open a checking and savings account for the student as soon as the student begins to work. It is advised to save 70% of their paycheck for college. Now is the time to learn these skills.

Start Working

Start them slow during the freshman year and slowly increase. See Chapter 15, page 144 for complete charts of suggested high school employment. A calculator is also available on www.CollegeSurvivorBook.com in the University of Success section to get a view of how much money your high school student can make and save. You will be able to enter any wage, and the calculator will do the work for you.

Work builds character. Your child can only benefit from this life experience, and it will prepare them for the transition to college.

Countdown to College: 24 Months

Junior Year, Fall
(September to November)
Two Years Before College Starts

1. **Take the PSAT**: take the PSAT as a junior to practice for the SAT and qualify for the National Merit Scholarship program.

2. **Prepare for the SAT and/or ACT:** begin preparing for the SAT and/or ACT at the start of junior year.

3. **College Visits:** take time in the fall of your junior year to visit local colleges.

> ### Junior Year, Winter
> ### (December to February)
> ### One Year and Nine Months Before College Starts

1. **Take the SAT and/or ACT:** take the SAT and/or ACT for the first time in the winter of junior year. Test again the spring of junior year or fall of senior year.

2. **List of Target Colleges:** identify ten, and research, research, research!

> ### Junior Year, Spring
> ### (March to May)
> ### One Year and Six Months Before College Starts

1. **PSATSAT and/or ACT:** if you feel like you can improve on your initial winter SAT and/or ACT results, take the SAT and/or ACT for the second time in the spring of junior year.

2. **AP Exams:** an opportunity to earn college credit (May).

> ### Junior Year, Summer
> ### (June to August)
> ### One Year and Three Months Before College Starts

1. **Know College Application Deadlines:** early decision and early action applications are typically due in November of your senior year.

2. **Recommendation Letters:** make a list of the teachers who will give you the best recommendations. These should be teachers from your core classes (Math, Science, History, English, or World Languages).

3. **Prep materials for Your Teachers' Letters of Recommendation:** your teachers need some guidance. Give them as much info as possible.

4. **Calculate Your Financial Gap:** *College Survivor* Calculators-www.collegesurvivobook.com, University of Success section.

Senior Year, Fall
(September to November)
One Year Before College Starts

1. **SAT and/or ACT**: if you desire an improvement on your initial SAT and/or ACT results, take the tests for the second (or at most, third) time in the fall of senior year.

2. **Letters of Recommendation**: at least a month prior to the deadline. Make sure they sign in ink and send you the original. Every College and Scholarship application has different requirements.

3. **Gather all Application Materials**: for college admissions, these include forms, test scores, essays, recommendations, and transcripts.

4. **Early Decision Application:** (optional and based on your decision.) Early decision applications, usually due in November, require a binding commitment in exchange for early acceptance.

5. **Early Action Applications**: for early action schools, you receive a decision early but can wait for the regular decision deposit deadline to make your final choice.

6. **FAFSA**: on or after October 1st.

Senior Year, Winter
(December to February)
180 to 270 Days Before College Starts

1. **Early Applications:** you should be notified within this time period.

2. **Financial Aid Package**: you should be notified within this time period. Most applications submitted through early programs will receive a decision by December. If you submit your financial aid forms on time, you should receive an estimated financial aid package as well.

3. **Submit Regular Decision Applications**: most colleges have regular decision due dates sometime between January 1st and March 1st of each year.

Senior Year, Spring
(March to May)
90 to 180 Days Before College Starts

1. **Update Your FAFSA**: revise your financial aid applications with data from your most recent year tax returns if this information was estimated on your initial FAFSA.

2. **Be Prepared to Send Transcripts and Documents:** certain colleges may require verification of your financial information.

3. **Receive Decision On Regular Applications**: regular decision applicants will receive an accept/reject/wait-list response in March or April.

4. **Compare Financial Aid Packages from Multiple Schools**: colleges will offer a financial aid package consisting of grants along with suggested loans and work-study. Sit down and compare. Make a pro vs. con list.

5. **Work-study**: sit down and compare the amount of money you can make at a local job. It is most likely more than work-study. However, if you are properly subsidized with scholarships and grants and have an opportunity to work directly in your field of study, it may be worth your time and dedication. Weigh the pros and cons.

6. **Loans**: if you do not a have scholarships or a financial plan in place, this will be your only option.

7. **Financial Aid Appeal**: life happens. Be Loud! If your family's circumstance has changed, contact your financial aid office ASAP to appeal the offer.

8. **Enrollment Deposit:** usually around May 1st.

9. **AP Exams:** AP Exams for college credit, usually around May 1st.

Senior Year, Summer
(June to August)
0 to 90 Days Before College Starts

1. **Stay on Top of Paperwork for Your College**: complete all paperwork by deadlines.

2. **Work-study Job Search**: if you have decided to pursue the work-study program, get ahead of the crowd. Coordinate with the financial aid office to determine options. Finalize your job search the summer before college begins.

NOTES

Resources available at
www.CollegeSurvivorBook.com / University of Success section!
Remember! Believe in Yourself! You've Got This

"Every time you fall down, you learn to pick yourself up. If someone is always there to break your fall, you will never learn how to pick yourself up and survive."

P. Friederich, single-parent college student

CHAPTER 11
WHAT IF?
HERE'S THE PROBLEM! WHAT IS YOUR SOLUTION?

> *"Children must be taught how to think,*
> *not what to think."*
> *--Margaret Mead*

In This Chapter

1. Note to parents
2. Note to college students
3. How does it work?
4. "What if" role-play questions

Note to Parents

High school students transitioning to college will be faced with adult situations on a daily basis. As a parent, you can help your child with the solution process before they transition.

Note to College Students

If you are an independent student without parental help, this is a great practice for you and your Dream Team.

How Does it Work?

The mentor (parent or older fellow student) should ask the question and the new or future student(s) should answer the question.

The role of the mentor is to coach and guide the student(s) to the best solution, not answer the question outright. After asking and solving each problem, ask the following questions.

1. Does your answer solve the situation?

2. Could you have prevented the situation?

3. Now that you have solved the problem, what is your plan B in case it happens again?

4. What did we learn from this situation?

5. Do you have any questions?

6. Can you handle this on your own?

What If?

SITUATION: You worked all summer and you are settling in. You have saved $3000. You are moving into your new apartment with your best friend. What expenses do you expect? How much do you think they will cost?

SITUATION: Everything is going great, but then your roommate has an unexpected family emergency and has to move home. They are unable to pay their half of the living expenses. What do you do? What is your plan B?

SITUATION: A person runs into your car and leaves the scene. Your car is completely totaled. What do you do? Now you do not have transportation!

SITUATION: You caught the flu and do not work for seven days. You have missed class and work. What do you do?

SITUATION: You accidentally tap a car while trying to park. No one is looking. You do not see any damage. What do you do?

SITUATION: You go to a party and as you are going to the bathroom, you see a door open with students doing drugs. What do you do?

SITUATION: You have lost your wallet and check your bank to find that someone has stolen your identity and your money. What do you do?

SITUATION: You go out with friends. After the party, the driver is drunk and will not give away the keys. What do you do?

SITUATION: You go out with friends and they decide to pull a prank on you. They drop you off in the middle of the country and take your phone. What do you do?

SITUATION: Your car breaks down in the middle of traffic. There is traffic everywhere and it is dangerous to get out of your car. Your phone is dead. What do you do?

SITUATION: You accidentally left your apartment or dorm room unlocked. When you return, your computer is gone. What do you do?

SITUATION: You have a flat tire with a dead phone and no road side assistance to help you. What do you do?

SITUATION: You run out of gas on a road with very few cars. Your phone is dead. What do you do?

SITUATION: You wake up with a 102 degree fever and think you have the flu. It is finals time. You have to take two finals today, one tomorrow and three the next day. What do you do?

SITUATION: Your roommate has a habit of wearing your clothes without asking. What do you do?

SITUATION: Your roommate asks to borrow money. What do you do?

SITUATION: During a test, the person sitting next to you continually looks at your answers and you are quite certain that they are cheating. What do you do?

SITUATION: Your professor returns your research paper and you receive a less than stellar grade. This is the first time that this has ever happened. What do you do?

SITUATION: You return to your apartment after work and find your roommate engaged in drug use. What do you do?

SITUATION: You are walking to your car after an evening class and a suspicious person is following you to your car. What do you do?

SITUATION: Your best friend tells you about criminal activity they were involved in. What do you do?

SITUATION: Your best friend is in dire straits due to an incident. They need you to comfort them, but the timing is difficult. It is finals time and you need to study. What do you do?

Add additional situations here.

Resources available at
www.CollegeSurvivorBook.com / University of Success section!
Remember! Believe in Yourself! You've Got This!

"During my daughter's sophomore year, she had two trips scheduled back to back within hours of each other. She arrived from a school trip, came home, showered, and packed for the next trip. She was home for three hours. I was concerned about sleep deprivation. Her answer to me was 'really mom, an object in motion tends to stay in motion. I have to stay in motion.' That day, I was schooled."

P. Solis-Friederich, the "just been schooled" mom

CHAPTER 12
A BALANCED LIFE, A HAPPY LIFE!
STRATEGY FOR RE-BALANCE

Newton's 1st Law
"Every object persists in its state of rest or uniform motion in a straight line unless it is compelled to change that state by forces impressed on it."

In This Chapter

❖ **Imbalance Check**

1. Academics

2. Employment

3. Skipping meals

4. Worry

5. Playtime

6. Sleep

7. Time management skills

8. Self-evaluation

❖ **Re-balance Strategy**

1. Academics

2. Employment

3. Play

4. Retrain the brain

❖ **Time Block Management**

1. What is Time Block Management
2. Your job as a student
3. A balanced week during an academic year
4. Time Block Management on a very challenging day

This chapter is designed to find out if you are in motion or at rest, and which factor is causing your imbalance if you are at rest. This is a precursor to *College Survivor Strategy*. The discovery process in this chapter will assist you in finding how to keep moving if you are in motion, and if you are at rest, in finding out why you are not moving and get you moving. The trick is finding out which unbalanced force in your life is keeping you from staying in motion. We will find it and crush it!

Imbalance Check

Are You In Motion?

Let's start now. Let's do a quick check to see if you are balanced. If you are balanced, then you are in motion. If you are unbalanced, then a simple adjustment will get you back on the road so you can become a *College Survivor*.

Consider this analogy. Imagine your car needs new tires. The new tires must be perfectly aligned and balanced, or you risk the performance and efficiency of your car. If your tires are unbalanced, then so are you. Make sense?

Car = You

Tires = Your Life

Do Any of These Issues Have an Impact on Your Balance?

Issue # 1: Too Many Academic Hours

Some students sign up for too many classes (17 to 19 hours) and become overwhelmed. In fact, at most colleges, a special approval is required by a student's dean of academics because of the academic workload. There are only so many hours in the day. A student may feel that taking a heavier load will help them graduate earlier. There is a backlash to this: burnout, fatigue, not enough hours to complete assignments, not enough time for quality study, etc. Worst of all, there may be no time for employment, playtime, and just relaxing and decompressing. And since there is no time for employment, loans may be the only option. Yeah, you graduated earlier, but the GPA suffered, and now you owe money! This situation spells disaster. The solution? Your academic advisor should assist you with a balanced academic schedule.

Issue #2: Not Enough Academic Hours

Students signing up for 12 hours or less are simply postponing graduation. And what about the cost? If a student goes to school for six years (example) and is working a college job for the entire time, they have given up two years of a professional salary. That's thousands and thousands of dollars. Ouch! And what about those pursuing a two-year degree at a community college? I have met many students that have taken four years to get a two-year degree and continue to work the college job. In the same sense, these extra two years represent a loss of a professional salary. Again, thousands of dollars are lost. And you can't turn back the clock! The solution? Same as above. Your academic advisor should assist you with a balanced academic schedule.

Issue #3: Choice of Employment

Your time is precious. Many students do not understand the concept of the best bang for their buck. Why are students spending their valuable time working a low-paying job with non-flexible hours? Your college job is only temporary. You are worth more than minimum wage. A person gets paid for every sixty minutes that they work. Trust me, there is another student working the same sixty minutes and making more money. In some cases, you might have to work ninety minutes to catch up with the sixty minutes of the other student's work. Think about it. If you have a low-paying job, you are still working while the other student is studying or enjoying playtime. Work smart, not hard. This will transcend into your future career. Master this art now! Find a job that gives you the most money for your effort. Pay yourself 10% for playtime. Save 10% for emergencies and use 80% for college fees and bills. There is a simple formula: make the most money in the shortest amount of time. Then, focus on the important things like class, sleeping, friends, and enjoying your college experience.

Issue #4: Skipping Meals

With a heavy school load, work load, and extra-curricular load, students begin to forget meals. Remember the analogy about the car and how you are the car?

Well, if you forget to put gas in the car, what happens? This is not a trick question! Pack healthy snacks in your backpack and graze all day long. Stay hydrated. And try to stay away from junk food if you can. Junk food tastes good, but it's not so healthy, right? During meals, put the phone down and talk to friends. Yes, talk. That is what my generation did. Your brain needs to know that you are eating. If you are busy watching cat videos (I actually love cat videos), your brain is still on electronic stimulation mode. Give your poor brain a break and feed your body real food.

Issue #5: Worry

The greatest worry is about paying rent and the impending college loan in addition to academic performance. Anyone can tell you to stop worrying, but it is honestly easier said than done. It is a mindset. You are in charge of your mindset.

First, let's get the mindset issue out of the way. Repeat this mantra: "I will not worry about things I cannot control." Here is where *College Survivor Strategy* can help you. If you have a solid plan for scholarships and grants and you execute the plan, what do you think happens? Less stress and anxiety lead to less worry, and a happier student.

Issue #6: Too Much Playtime

Have you ever looked up from your computer, tablet, or smartphone only to find that hours have passed, you are hungry, and your body has not even moved? You have been sedentary non-stop for all that time. And for guys, have you actually grown a beard while binge-watching a really awesome TV series? Just one more episode, just one more episode. I have done that too! Work hard and play hard. Both are important for balance. But if you play harder than you work (employment and academics), then you have an imbalance. If electronics are an issue, set a timer on your phone. Reduction is realistic; elimination is not.

Issue #7: Sleep Deprivation

There is absolutely no reason why any student should be sleep-deprived unless they have a newborn baby and are up all night. Sleep deprivation can lead to being late to class, skipping class, sleeping through class, and impacting the ability to focus on a task. Sleep deprivation can impact the GPA and possibly lead to cancelling paid classes to save the GPA. On the backend, cancelled classes become more expensive because then the student must pay a second or even third time to retake the same required class to satisfy graduation requirements. If you are sleep deprived, it is because there is imbalance.

Issue #8: Lack of Time Management Skills

Time management is something that is taught. No one is born with time management skills. Have you ever said, "I don't have time," "I wish I had more time," or "Where did the time go?" Learn how to manage your time. *College Survivor* is here to teach you. Go to page 106 for time block management coaching.

SELF-EVALUATION

There are only twenty-four hours in the day. How you use them will determine if you are a *College Survivor*. If you can master time, you will do very well in your career and have a balanced life.

So, now you have determined one or more imbalances in your life. Check the ones that apply:

- ☐ Academic Load
- ☐ Choice of Employment
- ☐ Skipping Meals
- ☐ Worry
- ☐ Too Much Playtime
- ☐ Sleep Deprivation

Which one is the biggest challenge for you? Why?

Now that you have read the issues that cause imbalance, ask yourself the following questions:

Are you in motion or are you at rest? (Hint: Are you busy or on your sofa?)

Your Answer:

Is there an external force in your life that causes you to become unbalanced that you **can control**? (Hint: These are things you can control—social media, friends, etc.)

Your Answer:

Is there an external force in your life that causes you to become unbalanced that you **cannot control**? (Hint: These are things that come into your life and force you to make decisions—a.k.a. peer pressure!)

Your Answer:

Re-balance Strategy

Balancing the Unbalanced

1. Academic re-balance.

2. Employment re-balance.

3. Play re-balance

4. Retrain the brain!

Academic re-balance

Balance the week as best as possible. Schedule three classes on Monday, Wednesday, and Friday, and two on Tuesday and Thursday. This is the perfect formula if you can get the classes you want. Classes all day on Tuesday and Thursday will wear you out. Try to stay away from overloading your schedule on certain days. Have classes on weekends as long as there is balance during the rest of the week. Make sure you have a designated day off, so you can decompress. Summer classes are good for catch-up, or if you need to retake a class. Another good strategy is to take your hardest class in the summer. This way, you can focus 100% on the class and get a better grade. Summer classes tend to be smaller and less overwhelming.

Employment re-balance

During the academic year, work no more than twenty-four hours per week (example: four to five hours per day for five days). You have thirty-five weeks to keep the money flowing. This leaves you two days to meet with your Dream Team. In the summer, work up to thirty-nine hours (example: seven or eight hours per day, five days per week). You have thirteen weeks to make bank. Your job during the summer is to work the hours, save properly, meet with your Dream Team, and play.

College Student Paycheck – 12 Months (1 year)

48 weeks per year / 4 weeks off for school activities, finals, holiday, illness

Academic year, 24 hour work week (35 weeks per year)

Summer, up to 39 hour work week (13 weeks per year)

Fund Allocation: 10% Play / 10% Emergency / 80% College Bills

Job Description	Summer/ Academic Yr.	Wage	hours per week	# Weeks	$ Net Per Week (after taxes)	$ Net per Summer or Academic Yr. (after taxes)	$ Net Per Yr. (after taxes)
Fast Food	Summer	$7.50	24	13	$135.00	$1,755.00	Fast Food
	Academic Yr.	$7.50	39	35	$219.38	$7,678.13	**$9,433.13**
Cashier	Summer	$8.90	24	13	$160.20	$2,082.60	Cashier
	Academic Yr.	$8.90	39	35	$260.33	$9,111.38	**$11,193.98**
Grocery 1*	Summer	$9.75	24	13	$175.50	$2,281.50	Grocery 1
	Academic Yr.	$9.75	39	35	$285.19	$9,981.56	**$12,263.06**
Grocery 2**	Summer	$10.75	24	13	$193.50	$2,515.50	Grocery 2
	Academic Yr.	$10.75	39	35	$314.44	$11,005.31	**$13,520.81**
Major Store	Summer	$11.50	24	13	$207.00	$2,691.00	Major Store
	Academic Yr.	$11.50	39	35	$336.38	$11,773.13	**$14,464.13**
CNA***	Summer	$12.50	24	13	$225.00	$2,925.00	CNA
	Academic Yr.	$12.50	39	35	$365.63	$12,796.88	**$15,721.88**
Waiter****	Summer	$15.00	24	13	$270.00	$3,510.00	Waiter
	Academic Yr.	$15.00	39	35	$438.75	$15,356.25	**$18,866.25**

*Grocery 1 – entry level job at a grocery store. ** Grocery 2 – promoted job at a grocery store. *** CNA – Certified Nursing Assistant. ****Waiter / waitress wages based on Iowa average of $5 wage per hour + $10 per hour tips = $15.00 zper hour

Play re-balance

There are numerous studies that show how much time we spend on our smartphones, tablets, and computers. Here's what we are doing daily on our smartphones. Ready for your smartphone statistics? This does not include the laptop and tablet!

- ❖ Mobile Internet Only (average of three studies, 2017—age 18 to 24):
- ❖ 4 hours 57 minutes per day / 155 hour per month / 1,825 hours per year

Here's what we are doing daily on our smartphones and social media(average of 5 studies, 2016 / 2017):

YouTube	Facebook	Snapchat	Instagram	Twitter
41 minutes	34 minutes	27 minutes	16 minutes	3 minutes

Even more interesting…in your whole lifetime, you will do the following (average of 4 studies):

Watch TV	Social Media	Eat/Drink	Grooming	Socializing	Laundry
7yrs, 8.1 mo.	5yrs, 4.3 mo.	3yrs, 5.0 mo.	1yr, 10.7 mo.	1yr, 3.2 mo.	5.9 mo.

No wonder a student forgets to eat. They spend more time on social media than nutrition.

Now that we know what we do, the question is: how can we use this time to be more productive? It works for us and against us.

Let's master this, guys!

Retrain the Brain

The reward for hard work is play. Play is very important and a great stress-reliever. Socializing and taking a break from academics and employment is very critical to balance. The current generation plays first, then works. Older generations would work first and play as a reward for their efforts. This is very difficult to relearn. So, create a new habit. A new habit takes two to three weeks of repetition. Here is an example of how you can change your mindset and behavior pattern.

Instructions: Think. Write. Commit.

Old Play Habit	New Play Habit
I will do my assignments after I….	After I do my assignments, I will be rewarded with….

Old Smartphone Habit	New Smartphone Habit
Track your minutes for 1 week or review your cell phone bill.	After you have determined your minutes per week, reduce by 20%. Divide your weekly minutes by 7 days then multiply x .8 and divide by 7. This is your new daily goal. Then set a daily timer on your phone. The goal is to reduce, not to eliminate. Don't forget to reward yourself!
Old Scheduling Habit	**New Scheduling Habit**
I will just remember everything.	Find a scheduling app that you like. There are many to choose from. DO: enter information in real time—that means NOW! DO NOT: say "I'll put in the information later." You will forget or lose important details about an assignment or incorrectly enter the wrong due date because you are relying on your memory. Let the app do the work for you.

Time Block Management

TIME IS FREE,

but it is priceless.

You can't own it,

but you can use it!

You can't keep it,

but you can spend it!

Once you've lost it

you can never get it back.

--Harvey MacKay

What Is Time Block Management?

A commitment to achieving certain goals within small portions of time.

How do you spend your time? There are only twenty-four hours in the day. What do you do with these precious hours? You have not entered the land of adulthood yet. You only have a few tasks that are important. Just wait until you have work deadlines, kids, spiritual activities (your choice), a house to manage, car management, medical bills, volunteering, and clubs, just to mention a few.

Your Job as a Student

1. Eat, drink, and sleep

2. Go to class, do your assignments, and study

3. Work

4. Play

5. Manage your money

Only five things to manage and you have twenty-four hours each day to do this. You can do this very successfully and enjoy life. College years are the best! Master time and the world is yours.

First, let's see what you do with your time then let's adjust it. You are in charge of the clock, not anyone else. Statistics say, over and over, that college students sleep an average of 8.8 hours per day. I was so happy to find this statistic in my research, because after reading so much propaganda about college student sleep deprivation, I reversed my beliefs and found out the truth.

So, what exactly do we do with our time? Play and procrastinate. Let's be honest. We all do this. But there is a time for work and a time for play. This is called balance. You will be happier and healthier and have a better GPA.

A Balanced Week During an Academic Year.

Who can hold you accountable? You!

How do you manage a day? Do you forget to turn in assignments? Can you remember everything? Well, who can? It is not your brain's job to remember everything. If you are trying to do this, no wonder you are overwhelmed. Not only are you overworking your body, you are overworking your brain. Find an app that tracks your assignments and work schedule and will alert you. This is your technology brain.

In the old days, we walked around with paper planners. But your generation does everything on the smartphone. Why do you think they call it smart? If you lose your phone, make sure you can access the app from your computer. Your only responsibility is to enter the data. Your phone cannot do it for you. The system will fail you if you fail the system. If you do not mind the paper method, get a planner that fits perfectly in your backpack. Use a pencil so you can erase when needed.

It is impossible to provide a perfect example because all students have different academic schedules and work schedules. The key to success is balance. This is a suggestion:

Day	Time	Activity
Mon - Fri	8:00AM to 3:00PM	Classes, with study in between. Get it done and over with.
	4:00PM to 10:00PM	Employment. Make the most money during this time.
	10:30PM to 7:00AM	Mon – Thurs & Sun – Bed Early and Fri - Sat Socialize / Enjoy your College Years!
Sat - Sun	10:00AM	Get up. Try not to oversleep past 10:00AM or your internal clock will cause you to think you are sleep deprived.
	12:00PM to 4:00PM	Meet with your *College Survivor* Dream Team at maximum 3 times per month with one weekend off per month.
	5:00PM to ?	If you are caught up on all your classes, this is your day off to decompress. If not, schedule your studies. The reward for accomplishing your studies is to play and socialize. If you do not accomplish your studies, then no reward.

Time Block Management on a very challenging day

Let's say this is a Wednesday, and your classes are spread out all day and you have to work at night. Plus, it is the only day that your study group can meet and the only day that your Dream Team can meet. This is a very long day. Eat, and stay hydrated and focused! Remember this is just one day of seven. You have six more days to conquer academics. But that doesn't mean you don't have to work hard rather than work smart, right?

What Do You Do With Your Time? This Is Your Decision!

Hour	BALANCED	UNBALANCED
	Working Smart	*Working Hard*
8:00AM - 9:30AM	Class #1	Class #1
9:30AM - 10:30AM	Break, travel, errands, and homework	Play
10:30AM - 12:00PM	Work on project with study group (eat and work).	Skip the group and play.
12:00PM - 12:30PM	Break, travel, errands, and homework.	Even more play
12:30PM - 1:00PM	Class #2	Class #2
1:00PM - 2:00PM	Break, travel, errands, and homework.	Nap – because you are exhausted
2:00PM - 3:00PM	Class #3	Class #3
3:00PM - 5:00PM	*College Survivor* Dream Team meeting (eat and work).	Skip the meeting and nap because you are exhausted.
5:00PM - 6:00PM	Decompress Time and prep for work	Decompress Time and prep for work
6:00PM - 10:00PM	Work 4 hours	Work 4 hours
10:00PM - 10:30PM	Travel home	Out with friends
10:30PM - 11:00PM	Decompress Time / Bed	Out with friends
12AM	Asleep	Finally get home and discover that an assignment is due that could have been accomplished earlier in the day. Work on the assignment till 3 a.m. Yikes! Now you will get four hours of sleep! Exhausted again.

What did you notice in the above example? The balanced side is well-rested and on task. The unbalanced side is exhausted, because of poor decision-making, and has created a destructive cycle. Ouch! Which side do you think has a better GPA, is healthier, and is happier? So, now you have accomplished everything. You have worked the twenty-four-hour maximum. You have completed all the academics, and you are a *College Survivor*. The cherry on top is the fact that your phone is doing all the remembering for you and you are less overwhelmed. Did you ever think it would be that easy? Caution: veer from the formula, and you will become unbalanced and overwhelmed! Play too much and disregard academics and work—disaster!

NOTES

Resources available at
www.CollegeSurvivorBook.com / University of Success section!
Remember! Believe in Yourself! You've Got This

"It can be lonely when taking on a project by yourself. Surround yourself with a powerful team and not only will you thrive, but your team will thrive!"

P. Solis-Friederich, team player

CHAPTER 13
THE DREAM TEAM
TEAMWORK ALWAYS PREVAILS!

> *"Talent wins games,*
> *but teamwork and intelligence win*
> *CHAMPIONSHIPS!*
> *--Michael Jordan*

In This Chapter

1. What is a Dream Team?

2. Why should I join a Dream Team?

3. Who are the members of the Dream Team?

4. Dream Team's first meeting

5. Parent Dream Team

6. College Student Dream Team

What Is a Dream Team?

A Dream Team consists of four members with individual traits that bring power and unity to your group. When your Dream Team gathers for a meeting, an amazing thing happens. If someone is down, the rest of the group perks the person up. If one person is having trouble on the internet or does not understand something, there is usually a teammate to help. And best of all, when applying for scholarships, your teammates may stumble upon a scholarship that does not work for their situation but is perfect for yours.

In fact, as you enter specific scholarship sites, a domino effect begins. All of a sudden, there are two to five more scholarships that you did not know existed. Provided they are not scams, you add them to your list and share your findings with your teammates. If you are using the book method (my preference), all the information is right in front of you. Then you can go to the scholarship website for updates.

Why Should I Join a Dream Team?

You need a support system. Can you do this alone? Yes! But you will be more successful in a team environment. Make it fun. Find a way to create hype. Help each other and approach it as if this were the only way to fund an education. The payout will be monumental. Your team is taking on a huge project! All four of you are using your resources to earn educational funds. Take this very seriously.

Who are the Members of the Dream Team?

The CEO

The CEO plays the role of visionary and leader. The greatest skill of the CEO is that they can take a project from the start to the finish and are able to resolve problems along the way. They are able to see the bigger picture, and this is crucial when it comes to bringing together different roles for the same project. The CEO is also a natural mentor. They are able to use their natural skills to motivate and encourage their teammates to meet deadlines and realize their true potential.

The Idea Guru

Idea gurus are innovators. They are incredibly valuable to a team, but they need the right management to make sure they aren't creating chaos on a project. Their natural talent is coming up with new ideas and different ways of doing things, and they can bring a breath of fresh air to any team. It is recommended that they work closely with the CEO to ensure all suggestions are staying on task for the group.

The Communication Specialist

The communication specialist has strong people skills and can use this to effectively interact with other team members. They are often the glue that holds the team together. The communication specialist naturally wants to make sure everyone is up to date with what's going on with the project and any new findings.

The Analyst

Analysts should work closely with the idea guru to find new and more effective methods for the Dream Team to operate. They are able to see problems, which means they also work well with the CEO to ensure any potential pitfalls are avoided. The analyst has strong problem-solving skills and should have the autonomy to make decisions for the team.

Tip

Make sure that you have the right personalities in your team. Possible failed teams would include too many CEOs and conflict with leadership. Another problem could be that you are missing a specific personality. It is just like a puzzle. If you are missing one piece, the entire puzzle is incomplete.

The Dreams Team's First Meeting

The Dream Team's first meeting is crucial. This is the foundation. One thing that is significant is the mindset. It is imperative that all team members agree on a common mindset so that all team members think alike. This creates ownership of the project.

1. Determine each person's role.

2. Determine if you are missing a specific personality and make a plan to find that person.

3. Set ground rules such as:

    a. No social media.

    b. Leave phones in the car or turn them off (vibrate does not count).

    c. No drama.

    d. Babysitting solutions (parents).

4. Agree on the mindset.

5. Plan and commit to your meeting dates and be realistic!

6. Set consequences for letting the team down.

7. Have a waiting list of people to replace a team member.

Notes

My list of potential Dream Team candidates:

1.

2.

3.

4.

Additional Rules:

1.

2.

3.

Parent Dream Team

What About Your Dream Team?

Your Dream Team will be your peers, co-workers, or long-time friends. Go through your contact list in your smartphone and determine the best parent friends with the right personalities to create your Dream Team. You are naturally aware of who is a leader and who is not. You are also aware of who you can count on and who will let you down. This team is for your children's education. It is okay to be "selective" or "picky."

What is Your Mindset?

If the mindset is that this project is a members-only club, the reward is a multitude of scholarships. And it is not likely that an adult would miss a club meeting. If the mindset is that of a part-time job, the payout is equivalent to a physician or attorney. Now that is a very nice part-time job! And an adult would not skip work.

What is Your Focus?

What did you think about Tony and Tina?

Refresh and take a second look at Chapter 3. Review each case study and think about the uniqueness of each situation. Tony and Tina are your children. How can you assist so they have the best situation? How can you assist so they can further their education as debt-free as possible?

What About Time?

What is the countdown till graduation? How many years? How many months? Do you have a plan? Time can be on your side with proper planning. You are at the beginning of your *College Survivor* road. Is your car ready? Is your smartphone charged? Do you have a map? Do you have a GPS or Map app on your smartphone with your destination ready to go? Take advantage of TIME, because you can never get it back!

College Student Dream Team

What About YOUR Dream Team?

Your Dream Team will be your friends and classmates. By now, you should be aware of which friends you can count on and which skills they can bring to your team. Be selective. This team is designed to help you with your journey for funding your education. Make every attempt to not include friends that you know you cannot count on. Your team is taking on a huge project! All four of you are using your resources to earn $80,000 to $100,000 as a team in just twelve months. Take this very seriously.

What is Your Mindset?

The Dream Team's first meeting is very important. This is the foundation. One thing that is very important is the mindset. It is essential that all agree that this project is either another class or a part-time job. Either way, there is ownership. If the mindset is that this project is another class, the reward is not a grade. The reward is a multitude of scholarships. If the mindset is that of a part-time job, the payout is equivalent to that of a physician or attorney. Now, that is a very nice part-time job!

What is Your Focus?

What did you think about Tony and Tina?

Refresh and take a second look at Chapter 3. Review each case study and think about the consequences for decisions. Will you work? Will you be a *College Survivor*? What are the possibilities of future debt? Do you understand how expensive debt can be on a monthly basis? Have you researched your potential career earning? If you have debt, can you afford to pay it? Really think about it. This is your life, and your decisions today will impact your pocketbook later!

What About Time?

Are you IN IT TO WIN IT? Time is on your side. You are at the beginning of your road. Is your car ready? Is your smartphone charged? Do you have a map finder with your destination ready to go? Take advantage of TIME, because you can never get it back!

NOTES

Resources available at
www.CollegeSurvivorBook.com / University of Success section!
Remember! Believe in Yourself! You've Got This

P. Solis-Friederich, B.A. Speech Communications

Texas A&M University, class of 1989.

K. Friederich, B.S. Economics and Business Administration

University of South Dakota, class of 1986

P. and K. Friederich, Attending the School of Hard Knocks of Parenting

University of Parenting, still waiting to graduate!

"I cannot believe that I have been a parent for thirty-two years. Three decades! 62% of my life has been dedicated to raising children 24/7/365—approximately 11,680 days. I have been blessed each and every second—1,009,152,000 seconds and counting!"

P. Solis-Friederich, the perpetual parent

CHAPTER 14
COLLEGE SURVIVOR STRATEGY
PARENT / MENTOR GUIDE

"If you want your children to turn out well,
spend twice as much time with them,
and half as much money."
--Abigail Van Buren

In This Chapter

1. Dear parent letter

2. Parents with multiple children

3. Twist—parent(s) returning to college

4. Your child's choice of career

5. Mentor Guide, step 1, situation, page 122

Hello, parents! You've got this! This is a mentor guide that supports chapter 15, *College Survivor Strategy* Step 1, Situation. You are the mentor. Without you, your child will have a more challenging transition to college. **Your mentor guide begins on page 122.**

Dear Parent,

I have the greatest respect for you. The fact that you are taking the time to help your child with scholarships shows a tremendous amount of love and character. Not all parents will take on this challenge, but you see this as an opportunity to assist your child in their future. I admire your dedication!

This chapter is written parent-to-parent. There are teaching videos, demonstrations, and resources available on www.CollegeSurvivorBook.com in the University of Success section that support every step of this book. It is my hope that you are very successful and are able to teach your children *College Survivor Strategy* so that they can continue it with their Dream Team while in college. Turning dreams into realities!

P. Solis-Friederich

Parents With Multiple Children

This is very challenging, to say the least. If you have multiple children, you will need to be very selective with your time.

A good example of a parent with multiple children would be a parent with four college-bound children—one in college, one in high school, one in middle school, and one in elementary. This is a tough situation. The college child needs money yesterday. The high school child needs to start filling their bank as soon as possible. The middle school and elementary children both have time, but their scholarships are the easiest and fastest to apply for. So, how do you approach this situation in the first year and the second year?

How do you allocate your time? Here is one suggestion:

Your Child's Grade Level	Year 1 First 6 months	Year 1 Second 6 months	Year 2 12 months
	% of your time per child	% of your time per child	% of your time per child
College	50%	20%	0%
High School	50%	60%	70%
Middle School	0%	15%	15%
Elementary School	0%	5%	10%

What Happened?

Year # 1 (first 6 months) You assisted your college child and high school child with *College Survivor Strategy* and you also coached them, so they can continue on their own.

Year #1 (second 6 months) You continued to assist the college child and high school child, but handed off the majority of the responsibility to your college child.

Year #2 (12 months) You continued to support your college child, but *College Survivor Strategy* is in their hands. You begin to assist your younger children at a higher percent.

Twist – parent(s) returning to college

Mom or Dad is back in school—now you have a real challenge! But it can be done! Your Dream Team may be your family. You know your family better than anyone else. Any of your children may or may not desire a further education, and you will have to decide where to allocate your time and effort.

Your child's choice of career

What to expect? National statistics indicate that 50% of students entering college are undecided, and that is okay. Once they start, they will find their way. When your child decides on an academic major, 50% to 70% will change their major at least three times before they graduate. It is important to know this and to be patient and supportive.

Your child may select their major for many reasons. Your child should choose a major directly related to their career choice, but in reality, most employers just want a degree in something. Can the high school guidance counselor provide a career/personality assessment? Yes! Are the results set in stone? No! The purpose of an assessment is to clarify strengths and weaknesses of your child. Ultimately, your child has passions and dreams, and such will determine their goals. Does a college degree guarantee career success? There are no guarantees in life. But a student with a college degree increases the odds of becoming gainfully employed vs. a student that does not have a degree.

Every Child deserves a Champion
An Adult who will never give up on them,
who understands the power of connection,
and insists that they can become
the best that they can possibly be.
– Rita F. Pierson

Mentor Guide

Step 1 - Situation

Step 1 - Situation, Chapter 15, Page 140

Mentors: your child's situation includes several financial evaluations. It is so important to help them understand their situation so that parent and child can proceed through step two, three, and four in College Survivor Strategy, Chapter 15. If you or your child do not understand the current situation, it is impossible to formulate a plan. The first step of College Survivor Strategy is the SITUATION.

Your situation includes several financial evaluations. It is so important to know and understand your situation so that you can proceed through steps two, three, and four. If you do not understand your current situation, it is impossible to formulate a plan. This is the first step of *College Survivor Strategy*.

Process for Determining Your Child's Situation

1. Goal setting

2. Consequences

3. Budget

   a. Income

   b. Expenses

4. Closing the Financial Deficit (gap)

5. Financial Deficit Calculator

6. Scholarship Deficit calculator

7. Commitment

Goal Setting – Chapter 15, Page 141

Mentors: *you are managing a business and developing a product to sell. The product is your college-bound child. You will spend a specified number of years developing this product so it is ready to take to market.*

Consider this analogy: When a new restaurant is opened for business, the owner has developed a plan for funding his project. The owner has also assured that the recipes are perfect, the atmosphere is just right, and the price points are on target. The owner has also found the right location and assembled a marketing plan. The owner has hired the best team of employees to assure success. The owner's employees are critical to his/her success, just like your Dream Team of parents and your child's Dream Team of friends.

Parent = Restaurant owner

Child = Restaurant

Consider this analogy. You are managing a business and developing a product to sell. The product is you. You will spend a specified number of years developing this product so it is ready to take to market for sale.

Example: When a new restaurant is opened for business, the owner has developed a plan for funding his project. He has also assured that the recipes are perfect, the atmosphere is just right, and the price points are on target. The owner has also found the right location and assembled a marketing plan. He has hired the best team of employees to assure success. His employees are critical to his success, just as your Dream Team is critical to your success. In it to win it!

You will begin with questions about passions and goals on the next page. Writing issues of the heart down makes it REAL. You now have ownership. Also, you may discover that you are majoring in, or planning on majoring in, a certain field that does not match your passion! Red flag! If you are Pre-Med for whatever reason, but pass out at the sight of blood, you are possibly not on track. Find your passion. You are the only one who knows and understands your personal passions. Turn that passion and dream into a goal!

It is recommended to write and date your answer in this book. Then repeat this action by writing or typing your passion in a place that you see every day such as your laptop, your screen saver on your phone, or on a sign. This is your business. This is your life. DO NOT TAKE IT FOR GRANTED! You literally get one chance to get this right the first time. It is a tough life lesson that many have learned. There are second chances, but life just gets in the way. Ask any adult or single parent headed back to school at an older age. YOU CAN DO THIS NOW!

Goal Setting, Chapter 15, Page 141

Mentors: *encourage your child to write down their own goals. This makes them real. This will create ownership. Have your child write it in this book (Chapter 15) and again in a place that they see every day, such as their laptop, screen saver on their phone, or on a sign. This is your child's life. Remind them to not take it for granted. Your child literally has one chance to get this right.*

Instructions: write your answer to each question listed below.

What is your passion?

Example: I love working with students.

What can you do with this passion?

Example: I can become a kindergarten teacher.

What are your dreams, if money were not an option?

Example: If I could do anything, I would open my own chain of preschools.

> **_Mentors:_** *now that your child has determined their passions and dreams, let's turn these passions and dreams into goals. In this example, this student is able to convert their passions into goals. Now, ask your child the same questions.*

So now that you have determined your passions and dreams, now let's determine your goals.

What are your goals?

Example: kindergarten teacher

How are you going to achieve your goals?

Example: I need a Bachelor's degree.

How long will it take to achieve these goals?

Example: It will take 4 years.

How much will it cost to achieve this goal (tuition, fees, books, living?)

Example: university choice #1 $150,000, university choice #2 $130,000

> ### Consequences – Chapter 15, Page 143
>
> **<u>Mentors:</u>** *If your child drops out, they have invested money into their product (themselves), and now your child owes money. Your child is not able to take their product to market. Their passion, dreams, and goals are just wishes. If they skip classes, they can expect a lower GPA that could diminish chances of graduating. In addition, they may have to drop out of a class and retake it. Now the cost of the class has doubled, and they have wasted their valuable time and hard earned money. For every action there is a result. Coach your child to find the right answer.*

This is the part that no one likes to talk about. The quick answer to the "consequences" question is "train wreck." If you drop out, you have invested money into your product (you), and now you owe money. You are not able to take your product to market. Your passion, dreams, and goals are just wishes. If you skip classes, you can expect a lower GPA that could diminish your chances of graduating. In addition, you may have to drop out of the class and retake it. Now the cost of the class has doubled, and you have wasted your valuable time and hard earned money. For every action there is a result. Here we go.

What are the consequences of dropping out of school?

(review Chapter 3, page 24)

What are the consequences of skipping class?

(review Chapter 12, page 108)

> ### Budget – Income – Chapter 15, Page 143
>
> **<u>Mentors:</u>** *your mentoring is critical during this process. These are adult evaluations. By assisting your college-bound child with understanding income and expenses, they will have a smoother adjustment to college. This will lead to less frustration and worry. We will begin the process of determining your child's future financial deficit (gap) by following a specific process. After determining the following resources below, then you will enter your information into the Financial Deficit Calculator and Scholarship Deficit Calculator available on www.CollegeSurvivorBook.com in the University of Success section. This will help you determine options to close the gap. Let's get started.*

Employment

❖ High School Student Paycheck – Summer Only vs. All Year

❖ College Student Paycheck – 1year, 2 years, 4 years

❖ High School and College Student Paycheck – 96 months, 8 years

❖ Income evaluation

❖ Determining your financial resources

❖ Parent Student Contract – refer to chapter 17

Your choice of employment can have a huge impact on your annual income and how it will fund your education. Many students will work a low paying job and sometimes two low paying jobs and not realize the impact. Money is tight, and they begin to work more jobs and more hours and sacrifice academics. Work smart! Not hard! So how does this effort add up over time?

Resources: High School Student Wage Projection and College Student Wage Projection calculators are available on www.CollegeSurvivorBook.com in the University of Success section to calculate earnings by year or by the balance of educational years. You will need this calculation to assist with determining your financial resources (income). Both are downloadable.

Employment – High School, Chapter 15, Page 144

Mentors: *talk about jobs! Your child's place of employment can have a huge impact on their income and how they will fund their education. Many students will work a low-paying job and not realize the impact. In high school, there are fewer demands for bills and financial commitments. Your child's bank can automatically take out a specific dollar amount or percentage of each check. Work smart! Not hard!*

Employment: High School - Summer versus 12 months

College Survivor Strategy recommends:

HS Paycheck – Summer Only

❖ 12 weeks per year

❖ Fund Allocation: 30% Play Money / 70% College Savings

HS Paycheck – 12 Months

❖ 44 weeks per year / 8 weeks off for school activities, holiday, illness

❖ Fund Allocation: 30% Play Money / 70% College Savings

HS Paycheck – Summer Only

Grade	Age	Wage	hours per wk.	$ Net Per Week (after taxes)	$ Net Per Yr. (after taxes)	30% Play Money	70% College Savings
H.S. Freshman	14 to 15	$7.50	15	$84.38	$1,012.50	$303.75	$708.75
H.S. Sophomore	15 to 16	$9.50	20	$142.50	$1,710.00	$513.00	$1,197.00
H.S. Junior	16 to 17	$11.50	30	$258.75	$3,105.00	$931.50	$2,173.50
H.S. Senior	17 to 18	$11.50	30	$258.75	$3,105.00	$931.50	$2,173.50
					$8,932.50	$2,679.75	$6,252.75

HS paycheck, summer only, chapter 15, page 144.

> **Mentors:** *a summer job is great for a freshman. But by the time your student is a sophomore, they should be ready to work all year. Only working in the summer is like only going to school on Monday and taking the rest of the week off. How much can a person learn on only one day of the week? Working is better than not working. A student who does not work at all will have the greatest struggle with the transition. They have not learned working social skills. It is best to work no matter the wage or the number of hours. The experience creates character.*

HS Paycheck – 12 Months

44 weeks per year / 8 weeks off for school activities, holiday, illness

Fund Allocation: 30% Play Money / 70% College Savings

Grade	Age	Wage	hours per wk.	$ Net Per Week (after taxes)	$ Net Per Yr. (after taxes)	30% Play Money	70% College Savings
H.S. Freshman	14 to 15	$7.50	10	$56.25	$2,475.00	$742.50	$1,732.50
H.S. Sophomore	15 to 16	$9.50	18	$128.25	$5,643.00	$1,692.90	$3,950.10
H.S. Junior	16 to 17	$11.50	20	$172.50	$7,590.00	$2,277.00	$5,313.00
H.S. Senior	17 to 18	$12.00	24	$216.00	$9,504.00	$2,851.20	$6,652.80
					$25,212.00	$7,563.60	$17,648.40

HS Paycheck, 12 months, chapter 15, page 144-145.

> ***Mentors:*** *a student who works all year builds momentum and trains their body to handle a variety of workloads. This student will have the easiest transition to college. They will have learned work ethic. They will have been mentored by a boss and learned the school of hard knocks at an early age. In a sense, these students are ahead of the curve when the time comes for graduation from high school. They have bought their own car, paid for their own cell phone, and learned simple budgeting. They are ready for the next level.*

> ***Employment: College – Chapter 15, Page 145***
>
> ***Mentors:*** *your child's place of employment can have a huge impact on their annual income and how it will fund their education. Many students will work a low paying job and sometimes two low paying jobs and not realize the impact. Money is tight, and they begin to work more jobs and more hours and sacrifice academics. Work smart! Not hard! So how does this effort add up over time?*

Employment: College, 1 year, 2 years, 4 years

College Survivor Strategy recommends:

- ❖ 48 weeks per year / 4 weeks off for school activities, finals, holiday, illness
- ❖ Academic year, 24 hour work week (35 weeks per year)
- ❖ Summer, up to 39 hour work week (13 weeks per year)
- ❖ Fund Allocation: 10% Play / 10% Emergency / 80% College Bills

College Paycheck – 1 year

Job Description	Summer/ Academic Yr.	Wage	hours per week	# Weeks	$ Net Per Week (after taxes)	$ Net per Summer or Academic Yr. (after taxes)	$ Net Per Yr. (after taxes)
Fast Food	Summer	$7.50	24	13	$135.00	$1,755.00	Fast Food
	Academic Yr.	$7.50	39	35	$219.38	$7,678.13	$9,433.13
Cashier	Summer	$8.90	24	13	$160.20	$2,082.60	Cashier
	Academic Yr.	$8.90	39	35	$260.33	$9,111.38	$11,193.98
Grocery 1*	Summer	$9.75	24	13	$175.50	$2,281.50	Grocery 1
	Academic Yr.	$9.75	39	35	$285.19	$9,981.56	$12,263.06
Grocery 2**	Summer	$10.75	24	13	$193.50	$2,515.50	Grocery 2
	Academic Yr.	$10.75	39	35	$314.44	$11,005.31	$13,520.81
Major Store	Summer	$11.50	24	13	$207.00	$2,691.00	Major Store
	Academic Yr.	$11.50	39	35	$336.38	$11,773.13	$14,464.13
CNA***	Summer	$12.50	24	13	$225.00	$2,925.00	CNA
	Academic Yr.	$12.50	39	35	$365.63	$12,796.88	$15,721.88
Waiter****	Summer	$15.00	24	13	$270.00	$3,510.00	Waiter
	Academic Yr.	$15.00	39	35	$438.75	$15,356.25	$18,866.25

*Grocery 1 – entry level job at a grocery store. ** Grocery 2 – promoted job at a grocery store. *** CNA – Certified Nursing Assistant. ****Waiter / waitress wages based on Iowa average of $5 wage per hour + $10 per hour tips = $15.00 per hour. College Paycheck, chapter 15, page 145.*

College Paycheck – 2 years

Job Description	24 months (2 years)	10% Savings	10% Play Money	80% College
Fast Food	$18,866.25	$1,886.63	$1,886.63	$15,093.00
Cashier	$22,387.95	$2,238.80	$2,238.80	$17,910.36
Grocery 1*	$24,526.13	$2,452.61	$2,452.61	$19,620.90
Grocery 2**	$27,041.63	$2,704.16	$2,704.16	$21,633.30
Major Store	$28,928.25	$2,892.83	$2,892.83	$23,142.60
CNA***	$31,443.75	$3,144.38	$3,144.38	$25,155.00
Waiter****	$37,732.50	$3,773.25	$3,773.25	$30,186.00

*Grocery 1 – entry level job at a grocery store. ** Grocery 2 – promoted job at a grocery store. *** CNA – Certified Nursing Assistant. ****Waiter / waitress wages based on Iowa average of $5 wage per hour + $10 per hour tips = $15.00 per hour. College Paycheck, chapter 15, page 145.*

College Paycheck – 4 years

Job Description	48 months (4 years) net after taxes	10% Savings	10% Play Money	80% College
Fast Food	$37,732.50	$3,773.25	$3,773.25	$30,186.00
Cashier	$44,775.90	$4,477.59	$4,477.59	$35,820.72
Grocery 1*	$49,052.25	$4,905.23	$4,905.23	$39,241.80
Grocery 2**	$54,083.25	$5,408.33	$5,408.33	$43,266.60
Major Store	$57,856.50	$5,785.65	$5,785.65	$46,285.20
CNA***	$62,887.50	$6,288.75	$6,288.75	$50,310.00
Waiter****	$75,465.00	$7,546.50	$7,546.50	$60,372.00

*Grocery 1 – entry level job at a grocery store. ** Grocery 2 – promoted job at a grocery store. *** CNA – Certified Nursing Assistant. ****Waiter / waitress wages based on Iowa average of $5 wage per hour + $10 per hour tips = $15.00 per hour. College Paycheck, chapter 15, page 145.

> ### *Employment: HS + College – Chapter 15, Page 146*
>
> **<u>Mentors:</u>** *this example shows how much money your child can save by working College Survivor Strategy from freshman in high school to senior in college.*

Employment: High School + College – 96 months, 8 Years

This example shows how much money you can save by working *College Survivor Strategy* from freshman in high school to senior in college.

HS Paycheck – 4 years + College Paycheck – 4 years = 8 years

Job Description	HS – 4 years Coll – 4 years net after taxes	Play Money HS 10% / Coll 10%	Savings / Emergency Coll 10%	College Savings HS 70% / Coll 80%
High School*	$25,212.00	$7,563.60	$0	$17,648.40
College**	$57,856.52	$5,785.65	$5,785.65	$46,285.22
Total=8 years	$83,068.52	$13,349.25	$5,785.65	$63,933.62

*HS paycheck, 12 months, chapter 15, page 144.**College paycheck, 4 years, chapter 15, page 146

Unfortunately, this sometimes happens...

HS Paycheck – 4 years + College Paycheck – 4 years = 8 years

Job Description	96 months (8 years) net after taxes	Play Money HS 100% Coll 25%	Savings / Emergency Coll 0%	College Savings HS 0% / Coll 75%
High School*	$25,212.00	$25,212.00	$0	$0
College**	$57,856.52	$14,464.13	$0	$43,392.39
Total=8 years	**$83,068.52**	**$39,676.13**	**$0**	**$43,392.39**

*HS paycheck, 12 months, chapter 15, page 144.**College paycheck, 4 years, chapter 15, page 146*

Income Evaluation – Chapter 15, Page 143

<u>Mentors:</u> *assist your child with decisions and resources The College Survivor employment calculator is available on www.CollegeSurvivorBook.com in the University of Success section to calculate earnings by year or by the balance of educational years. You will need this calculation to assist with determining your child's financial resources (income).*

Instructions:

On a separate piece of paper, begin to answer or estimate the financial questions. Next, go to <u>www.CollegeSurvivorBook.com</u> and select one of the budgeting links. Enter your information. This information is necessary for the Scholarship Deficit Calculator so that you may develop your plan.

Income Evaluation

☐ What is your child's current wage?

☐ What is your child's wage goal?

☐ Does your child plan to change jobs?

Determining Your Child's Financial Resources

☐ How much money will your child make from employment?

☐ How much money is available in savings and investment?

☐ Has your child been offered a financial package? (if applicable)

☐ Has your child been awarded scholarships?

☐ Does your child have funding from other sources?

> ### *Budget – Expenses – Chapter 15, Page 148*
>
> <u>*Mentors:*</u> *talk about expenses! Your child does not have the experience you have with paying bills. There are links available to the best budget calculators on www.CollegeSurvivorBook.com in the University of Success section. The sooner you can teach your child to budget, the better. Here are some items you need to gather so you can start budgeting. You will be ready for that dorm or first apartment in no time!*

Instructions:

Continue with your financial estimates and begin to estimate the budget expenses. Next, go to www. CollegeSurvivorBook.com and select one of the budgeting links. Enter your information. This information is necessary for the Scholarship Deficit Calculator so that you may develop your plan.

Budget Items (Examples)

- ❖ **College Expenses:** tuition, fees, books, supplies
- ❖ **Room and Board:** mortgage, rent, dorm package, gas, electric, insurance, other
- ❖ **Debts:** student loans, credit cards, bank loans, other
- ❖ **Charity:** faith organization, community
- ❖ **Transportation:** car purchase, tag/title/license, car payment, insurance, annual tags, car maintenance, tires, oil changes, public transportation, parking, shuttle pass,
- ❖ **Special Occasion:** birthday, anniversary, holiday
- ❖ **Medical:** insurance, co-pay, prescriptions, other
- ❖ **Pet:** purchase, vaccinations, maintenance, pet deposit
- ❖ **Communication:** cellphone purchase, monthly payment, Wi-Fi, accessories, other
- ❖ **Entertainment:** movies, video games, video rental, concerts, eating out, going out with friends, entertaining friends
- ❖ **Apps:** for school, for fun
- ❖ **Wardrobe:** clothing, shoes, coat, jacket, special occasion
- ❖ **Personal:** hygiene, haircuts, salon, other
- ❖ **Household:** cleaning items, cleaning tools, other

> ### *Closing the Financial Deficit (Gap) – Chapter 15, Page 149*
>
> <u>*Mentors:*</u> *together, work through the calculators available on <u>www.CollegeSurvivorBook.com</u> in the University of Success section.*

Financial Deficit Calculator

Now that you have gathered your information, there is a calculator available on <u>www.CollegeSurvivorBook.com</u> in the University of Success section that is designed for *College Survivors*. Once you have entered your income and expenses, this calculator will provide a clear picture of your financial deficit (gap).

This calculator can be used at any time. When there is a change in employment, if you move, or if you add or delete a roommate, the calculation will change. This is your gap. The next and most important step is the Scholarship Deficit Calculator. This calculator will evaluate your financial deficit (gap) and provide several options to close the gap. This is the beginning of the HOW—the missing link. The task section will provide a systematic way of organizing information, so you will be prepared for the action and results section in Chapter 15.

> ### *Scholarship Deficit Calculator, Chapter 15, Page 149*
>
> <u>*Mentors:*</u> *the example below will shed light on waiting until later. Here is your chance to make a very serious point!*

Scholarship Deficit Calculator

The Scholarship Deficit Calculator can be used at any time to track your progress. You will be asked several questions, and the calculator will provide options for a plan of execution. The most effective way to use this calculator is to enter information as soon as you receive your first scholarship check or award letter. This calculator is available in <u>www.CollegeSurvivorBook.com</u> in the University of Success Section.

Example: Review Chapter 3, Plan D, page 30

Tina answers several questions based on the results of her Financial Deficit Calculator, and the Scholarship Deficit Calculator provides the following options:

Average value of each scholarship = $750

Option #1

Meet with Dream Team four times per month for 3.2 hours per meeting and apply for two individual scholarships per meeting.

Option #2

Meet with Dream Team three times per month for 4.2 hours per meeting and apply for three individual scholarships per meeting.

Option #3

Meet with Dream Team two times per month for 6.3 hours per meeting and apply for four individual scholarships per meeting.

These options will assist Tina in closing her financial deficit. She will need to apply for scholarships that that have a value of at least $750. It is up to her to decide how many times per month to meet with her Dream Team. The information is designed with the expectation of earning 20% of scholarship applications.

In this example, Chapter 3, Plan D, page 30, indicates that Tina has a financial gap of $52,028.44. In order to close her financial gap, she will need to apply for $260,142.20 in scholarship applications over a four-year period and earn 20%. The options are calculated for Tina. Now it is her decision to commit. It is highly recommended to use the Scholarship Deficit Calculator because it is accurate and saves you time and energy so you can focus on academics and employment and not spend hours trying to reconfigure the plan.

> _**Mentors:** here is the opportunity to demonstrate how a large and overwhelming task can be achieved with a plan that includes small increments of time and effort with big results._

Does $260,142.20 seem like a lot of money? The Scholarship Deficit Calculator provides several options to achieve this hefty goal. Tina only needs $52,028.44 in 4 years to graduate debt fee. The calculator does the work for you. Essentially applying for $260,142.20 in four years is the same as applying for $5,419.63 every month. If Tina decides to meet with her Dream Team three times per month, she will apply for $1,806.54 per meeting. If her average scholarship application is $750, she will apply for 2.4 scholarships at each meeting. Tina has an expectation of winning 20% of the scholarships. 20% of $260,142.20 is $52,028.44. Goal! Debt Free! Make sense?

Commitment – Chapter 15, Page 150

Mentors: *help your child understand how to make a commitment and the consequences. Based on your child's results, what is their commitment and your commitment as a parent? A helpful document - Parent Student Commitment Contract is available online and on page 173.*

Example:

I need _____ in scholarship dollars and I will commit to meeting ___ times per month with my Dream Team for _____ hours to make this happen!

Mentors: *the following example of non-commitment is very powerful and eye-opening. Please discuss this scenario with your child.*

Excerpt from Chapter 3 – page 33

Many students decide to worry about it later, while others constantly worry but do not have a plan. When you worry about it later, you have to work harder. For example, in scenario #2, page 25, Tina did not work or apply for assistance. She lived completely on loans. She now owes $131,459.60 without interest.

What does this mean? How can a little planning and work payoff? Let's say Tina lands an incredible job, but she cannot afford her rent because of her college loans.

There are a couple of ways Tina can pay these loans.

1. Tina can move home for five to eight years and use her new income to pay for the loan.

2. Tina can live on her own with her new job and take on a second job on the weekends to pay for the college debt.

3. **Tina can work as a waitress with a wage of $15 per hour. She would need to work every Saturday and Sunday (seven-hour shift) for approximately 12 years. Additional years would be required for the interest on the loan.**

Mentors – *You have successfully completed Step 1 – Situation with your college –bound child. Next, you will proceed to page 151 to begin Step 2 –Task and then continue with the final steps – Step 3 – Action and Step 4 – Results.*

A Truly Great Mentor

Is hard to find

Difficult to part with

And

Impossible to Forget

-Anonymous

Resources available at
www.CollegeSurvivorBook.com / University of Success section!
Remember! Believe in Yourself! You've Got This!

"I always dreamed of traveling abroad as a college student. Follow your dreams!"

P. Solis-Friederich, the dreaming college student

CHAPTER 15
COLLEGE SURVIVOR STRATEGY
PARENT, MENTOR, HIGH SCHOOL, COLLEGE STUDENT

> *"You don't have to see the whole staircase,*
> *just take the first step."*
> *--Martin Luther King*

One of the oldest formulas that has been used for decades in business settings all over the world, the S.T.A.R. method, in conjunction with the team concept, is consistently successful because the process repeats itself over and over and becomes a fine-oiled machine. It works. It will always work.

We are going to take this college adventure one step at a time. There is a method to the madness. Trust the process. By the end of this chapter, you should feel full of energy and recharged, and should possibly have solved some soul-searching issues with the help of your Dream Team. You will have a solid plan. It will be up to you to execute the plan! Let's get ready to take on the day. Survive and thrive!

Important! If you skip a step, you have failed the process and the process will fail you. It is a proven fact. Let's Get Started! We have NO TIME TO WASTE!

In This Chapter

Step 1: Evaluate your SITUATION

Step 2: Determine your TASK

Step 3: Place your task into ACTION

Step 4: Evaluate your RESULT, then REPEAT

Track your winnings

Reflection

Situation, Step 1

Your situation includes several financial evaluations. It is so important to know and understand your situation so that you can proceed through steps two, three, and four. If you do not understand your current situation, it is impossible to formulate a plan. This is the first step of *College Survivor Strategy*.

Process for Determining Your Situation

1. Goal Setting

2. Consequences

3. Budget

   a. Income

   b. Expenses

4. Closing the Financial Deficit (Gap)

   a. Financial Deficit Calculator

   b. Scholarship Deficit Calculator

5. Commitment

Goal Setting

Consider this analogy. You are managing a business and developing a product to sell. The product is you. You will spend a specified number of years developing this product so it is ready to take to market for sale.

Example: When a new restaurant is opened for business, the owner has developed a plan for funding his/her project. He has also assured that the recipes are perfect, the atmosphere is just right, and the price points are on target. The owner has also found the right location and assembled a marketing plan. He/she has hired the best team of employees to assure success. His/her employees are critical to their success, just as your Dream Team is critical to your success. In it to win it!

You will begin with questions about passions and goals on the next page. Writing issues of the heart down makes it REAL. You now have ownership. Also, you may discover that you are majoring in, or planning on majoring in, a certain field that does not match your passion! Red flag! If you are Pre-Med for whatever reason, but pass out at the sight of blood, you are possibly not on track. Find your passion. You are the only one who knows and understands your personal passions. Turn that passion and dream into a goal!

It is recommended to write and date your answer in this book. Then repeat this action by writing or typing your passion in a place that you see every day such as your laptop, your screen saver on your phone, or on a sign. This is your business. This is your life. DO NOT TAKE IT FOR GRANTED! You literally get one chance to get this right the first time. It is a tough life lesson that many have learned. There are second chances, but life just gets in the way. Ask any adult or single parent headed back to school at an older age. YOU CAN DO THIS NOW!

Instructions: write your answer to each question listed below.

What is your passion?

Example: I love working with students.

What can you do with this passion?

Example: I can become a kindergarten teacher.

What are your dreams, if money were not an option?

Example: If I could do anything, I would open my own chain of preschools.

So now that you have determined your passions and dreams, now let's determine your goals.

What are your goals?

Example: kindergarten teacher

How are you going to achieve your goals?

Example: I need a Bachelor's degree.

How long will it take to achieve these goals?

Example: It will take 4 years.

How much will it cost to achieve this goal (tuition, fees, books, living?)

Example: university choice #1 $150,000, university choice #2 $130,000

Consequences

This is the part that no one likes to talk about. The quick answer to the "consequences" question is "train wreck." If you drop out, you have invested money into your product (you), and now you owe money. You are not able to take your product to market. Your passion, dreams, and goals are just wishes. If you skip classes, you can expect a lower GPA that could diminish your chances of graduating. In addition, you may have to drop out of the class and retake it. Now the cost of the class has doubled, and you have wasted your valuable time and hard earned money. For every action there is a result. Here we go.

What are the consequences of dropping out of school?

(review Chapter 3, page 24)

What are the consequences of skipping class?

(review Chapter 12, page 108)

Budget - Income

Employment

- ❖ High School Student Paycheck – Summer Only vs. All Year
- ❖ College Student Paycheck – 1year, 2 years, 4 years
- ❖ High School and College Student Paycheck – 96 months, 8 years
- ❖ Income evaluation
- ❖ Determining your financial resources
- ❖ Parent Student Contract – refer to chapter 17

Your choice of employment can have a huge impact on your annual income and how it will fund your education. Many students will work a low paying job and sometimes two low paying jobs and not realize the impact. Money is tight, and they begin to work more jobs and more hours and sacrifice academics. Work smart! Not hard! So how does this effort add up over time?

Resources: High School Student Wage Projection and College Student Wage Projection calculators are available on www.CollegeSurvivorBook.com in the University of Success section to calculate earnings by year or by the balance of educational years. You will need this calculation to assist with determining your financial resources (income). Both are downloadable.

Employment: High School - Summer versus 12 months

College Survivor Strategy recommends:

HS Paycheck – Summer Only

- ❖ 12 weeks per year
- ❖ Fund Allocation: 30% Play Money / 70% College Savings

HS Paycheck – 12 Months

- ❖ 44 weeks per year / 8 weeks off for school activities, holiday, illness
- ❖ Fund Allocation: 30% Play Money / 70% College Savings

HS Paycheck – Summer Only

12 weeks

Fund Allocation: 30% Play Money / 70% College Savings

Grade	Age	Wage	hours per wk.	$ Net Per Week (after taxes)	$ Net Per Yr. (after taxes)	30% Play Money	70% College Savings
H.S. Freshman	14 to15	$7.50	15	$84.38	$1,012.50	$303.75	$708.75
H.S. Sophomore	15 to16	$9.50	20	$142.50	$1,710.00	$513.00	$1,197.00
H.S. Junior	16 to17	$11.50	30	$258.75	$3,105.00	$931.50	$2,173.50
H.S. Senior	17 to18	$11.50	30	$258.75	$3,105.00	$931.50	$2,173.50
					$8,932.50	$2,679.75	$6,252.75

HS Paycheck – 12 Months

44 weeks per year / 8 weeks off for school activities, holiday, illness

Fund Allocation: 30% Play Money / 70% College Savings

Grade	Age	Wage	hours per wk.	$ Net Per Week (after taxes)	$ Net Per Yr. (after taxes)	30% Play Money	70% College Savings
H.S. Freshman	14 to 15	$7.50	10	$56.25	$2,475.00	$742.50	$1,732.50
H.S. Sophomore	15 to 16	$9.50	18	$128.25	$5,643.00	$1,692.90	$3,950.10
H.S. Junior	16 to 17	$11.50	20	$172.50	$7,590.00	$2,277.00	$5,313.00
H.S. Senior	17 to 18	$12.00	24	$216.00	$9,504.00	$2,851.20	$6,652.80
					$25,212.00	$7,563.60	$17,648.40

Employment: College, 1 year, 2 years, 4 years

College Survivor Strategy recommends :

❖ 48 weeks per year / 4 weeks off for school activities, finals, holiday, illness

❖ Academic year, 24 hour work week (35 weeks per year)

❖ Summer, up to 39 hour work week (13 weeks per year)

❖ Fund Allocation: 10% Play / 10% Emergency / 80% College Bills

College Paycheck – 1 year

Job Description	Summer/ Academic Yr.	Wage	hours per week	# Weeks	$ Net Per Week (after taxes)	$ Net per Summer or Academic Yr. (after taxes)	$ Net Per Yr. (after taxes)
Fast Food	Summer	$7.50	24	13	$135.00	$1,755.00	Fast Food
	Academic Yr.	$7.50	39	35	$219.38	$7,678.13	**$9,433.13**
Cashier	Summer	$8.90	24	13	$160.20	$2,082.60	Cashier
	Academic Yr.	$8.90	39	35	$260.33	$9,111.38	**$11,193.98**
Grocery 1*	Summer	$9.75	24	13	$175.50	$2,281.50	Grocery 1
	Academic Yr.	$9.75	39	35	$285.19	$9,981.56	**$12,263.06**
Grocery 2**	Summer	$10.75	24	13	$193.50	$2,515.50	Grocery 2
	Academic Yr.	$10.75	39	35	$314.44	$11,005.31	**$13,520.81**
Major Store	Summer	$11.50	24	13	$207.00	$2,691.00	Major Store
	Academic Yr.	$11.50	39	35	$336.38	$11,773.13	**$14,464.13**
CNA***	Summer	$12.50	24	13	$225.00	$2,925.00	CNA
	Academic Yr.	$12.50	39	35	$365.63	$12,796.88	**$15,721.88**
Waiter****	Summer	$15.00	24	13	$270.00	$3,510.00	Waiter
	Academic Yr.	$15.00	39	35	$438.75	$15,356.25	**$18,866.25**

*Grocery 1 – entry level job at a grocery store. ** Grocery 2 – promoted job at a grocery store. *** CNA – Certified Nursing Assistant. ****Waiter / waitress wages based on Iowa average of $5 wage per hour + $10 per hour tips = $15.00 per hour*

College Paycheck – 2 years

Job Description	24 months (2 years)	10% Savings	10% Play Money	80% College
Fast Food	$18,866.25	$1,886.63	$1,886.63	$15,093.00
Cashier	$22,387.95	$2,238.80	$2,238.80	$17,910.36
Grocery 1*	$24,526.13	$2,452.61	$2,452.61	$19,620.90
Grocery 2**	$27,041.63	$2,704.16	$2,704.16	$21,633.30
Major Store	$28,928.25	$2,892.83	$2,892.83	$23,142.60
CNA***	$31,443.75	$3,144.38	$3,144.38	$25,155.00
Waiter****	$37,732.50	$3,773.25	$3,773.25	$30,186.00

*Grocery 1 – entry level job at a grocery store. ** Grocery 2 – promoted job at a grocery store. *** CNA – Certified Nursing Assistant. ****Waiter / waitress wages based on Iowa average of $5 wage per hour + $10 per hour tips = $15.00 per hour*

College Paycheck – 4 years

Job Description	48 months (4 years) net after taxes	10% Savings	10% Play Money	80% College
Fast Food	$37,732.50	$3,773.25	$3,773.25	$30,186.00
Cashier	$44,775.90	$4,477.59	$4,477.59	$35,820.72
Grocery 1*	$49,052.25	$4,905.23	$4,905.23	$39,241.80
Grocery 2**	$54,083.25	$5,408.33	$5,408.33	$43,266.60
Major Store	$57,856.50	$5,785.65	$5,785.65	$46,285.20
CNA***	$62,887.50	$6,288.75	$6,288.75	$50,310.00
Waiter****	$75,465.00	$7,546.50	$7,546.50	$60,372.00

*Grocery 1 – entry level job at a grocery store. ** Grocery 2 – promoted job at a grocery store. *** CNA – Certified Nursing Assistant. ****Waiter / waitress wages based on Iowa average of $5 wage per hour + $10 per hour tips = $15.00 per hour*

Employment: High School + College – 96 months, 8 Years

This example shows how much money you can save by working *College Survivor Strategy* from freshman in high school to senior in college.

HS Paycheck (4 years) + College Paycheck (4 years) = 8 years

Job Description	HS – 4 years Coll – 4 years net after taxes	Play Money HS 10% / Coll 10%	Savings / Emergency Coll 10%	College Savings HS 70% / Coll 80%
High School*	$25,212.00	$7,563.60	$0	$17,648.40
College**	$57,856.52	$5,785.65	$5,785.65	$46,285.22
Total=8 years	$83,068.52	$13,349.25	$5,785.65	$63,933.62

Unfortunately, this sometimes happens...

HS Paycheck (4 years) + College Paycheck (4 years) = 8 years

Job Description	96 months (8 years) net after taxes	Play Money HS 100% Coll 25%	Savings / Emergency Coll 0%	College Savings HS 0% / Coll 75%
High School*	$25,212.00	$25,212.00	$0	$0
College**	$57,856.52	$14,464.13	$0	$43,392.39
Total=8 years	$83,068.52	$39,676.13	$0	$43,392.39

Instructions:

On a separate piece of paper, begin to answer or estimate the income financial questions. Next, go to www.CollegeSurvivorBook.com and select one of the budgeting links. Enter your information. This information is necessary for the Scholarship Deficit Calculator so that you may develop your plan.

Income Evaluation

☐ What is your current wage?

☐ What is your wage goal?

☐ Do you plan to change jobs?

Determining Your Financial Resources

☐ How much money will you make from employment?

☐ How much money is available in savings, investment?

☐ Have you been offered a financial package? (if applicable)

☐ Have you been awarded scholarships?

☐ Do you have funding from other sources?

147

Budget – Expenses

Instructions:

Continue with your financial estimates and begin to estimate the budget expenses. Next, go to www. CollegeSurvivorBook.com and select one of the budgeting links. Enter your information. This information is necessary for the Scholarship Deficit Calculator so that you may develop your plan.

Budget Items (Examples)

❖ **College Expenses:** tuition, fees, books, supplies

❖ **Room and Board:** mortgage, rent, dorm package, gas, electric, insurance, other

❖ **Debts:** student loans, credit cards, bank loans, other

❖ **Charity:** faith organization, community

❖ **Transportation:** car purchase, tag/title/license, car payment, insurance, annual tags, car maintenance, tires, oil changes, public transportation, parking, shuttle pass,

❖ **Special Occasion:** birthday, anniversary, holiday

❖ **Medical:** insurance, co-pay, prescriptions, other

❖ **Pet:** purchase, vaccinations, maintenance, pet deposit

❖ **Communication:** cellphone purchase, monthly payment, Wi-Fi, accessories, other

❖ **Entertainment:** movies, video games, video rental, concerts, eating out, going out with friends, entertaining friends

❖ **Apps:** for school, for fun

❖ **Wardrobe:** clothing, shoes, coat, jacket, special occasion

❖ **Personal:** hygiene, haircuts, salon, other

❖ **Household:** cleaning items, cleaning tools, other

Closing the Financial Deficit (Gap)

Financial Deficit Calculator

Now that you have gathered your information, there is a calculator available in www.CollegeSurvivorBook.com in the University of Success section that is designed for *college survivors*. Once you have entered your income and expenses, this calculator will provide a clear picture of your financial deficit (gap).

This calculator can be used at any time. When there is a change in employment, if you move, or if you add or delete a roommate, the calculation will change. This is your gap. The next, and most important, step is the Scholarship Deficit Calculator. This calculator will evaluate your financial deficit (gap) and provide several options to close the gap. This is the beginning of the *HOW*—the missing link. The task section will provide a systematic way of organizing information, so that you will be prepared for the action and results section in this chapter.

Scholarship Deficit Calculator

The Scholarship Deficit Calculator can be used at any time to track your progress. You will be asked several questions and the calculator will provide options for a plan of execution. The most effective way to use this calculator is to enter information as soon as you receive your first scholarship check or award letter. This calculator is available in www.CollegeSurvivorBook.com in the University of Success section.

Example: Review Chapter 3, Plan D, page 30

Tina answers several questions based on the results of her Financial Deficit Calculator and the Scholarship Deficit Calculator provides the following options:

Average value of each scholarship = $750

Option #1

Meet with Dream Team four times per month for 3.2 hours per meeting and apply for two individual scholarships per meeting.

Option #2

Meet with Dream Team three times per month for 4.2 hours per meeting and apply for three individual scholarships per meeting.

Option #3

Meet with Dream Team two times per month for 6.3 hours per meeting and apply for four individual scholarships per meeting.

These options will assist Tina in closing her financial deficit. She will need to apply for scholarships that that have a value of at least $750. It is up to her to decide how many times per month to meet with her Dream Team. The information is designed with the expectation of earning 20% of scholarship applications.

In this example, Chapter 3, Plan D, page 30, indicates that Tina has a financial gap of $52,028.44. In order to close her financial gap, she will need to apply for $260,142.20 in scholarship applications over a four-year period and earn 20%. The options are calculated for Tina. Now it is her decision to commit. It is highly recommended to use the Scholarship Deficit Calculator because it is accurate and saves you time and energy so you can focus on academics and employment and not spend hours trying to reconfigure the plan.

Does $260,142.20 seem like a lot of money? The Scholarship Deficit Calculator provides several options to achieve this hefty goal. Tina only needs $52,028.44 in 4 years to graduate debt fee. The calculator does the work for you. Essentially applying for $260,142.20 in four years is the same as applying for $5,419.63 every month. If Tina decides to meet with her Dream Team three times per month, she will apply for $1,806.54 per meeting. If her average scholarship application is $750, she will apply for 2.4 scholarships at each meeting. Tina has an expectation of winning 20% of the scholarships. 20% of $260,142.20 is $52,028.44. Goal! Debt Free! Make sense?

Commitment

Based on your results from the Scholarship Deficit Calculator, what is your commitment?

Example:

I need _____ in scholarship dollars and I will commit to meeting ____ times per month with my Dream Team for _____ hours to make this happen! I understand that my average scholarship application should be $750 or more to achieve my goal and close my financial deficit.

Excerpt From Chapter 3, Page 33

Many students decide to worry about it later while others constantly worry but do not have a plan. When you worry about it later, you have to work harder. For example: In Chapter 3, scenario #2, page 25, Tina did not work or apply for assistance. She lived completely on loans. She now owes $131,459.60 without interest.

What does this mean? How can a little planning and work payoff? Let's say Tina lands an incredible job, but she cannot afford her rent because of her college loans.

There are a couple of ways Tina can pay these loans.

1. Tina can move home for five to eight years and use her new income to pay for the loan.

2. Tina can live on her own with her new job and take on a second job on the weekends to pay for the college debt.

3. **Tina can work as a waitress with a wage of $15 per hour. She would need to work every Saturday and Sunday (seven-hour shift) for approximately 12 years. Additional years would be required for the interest on the loan.**

Task, Step 2

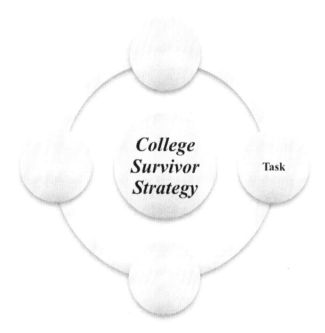

This is the preparation phase. The next step is #3: action. You will not be able to effectively execute action unless you are prepared.

You will request, gather, and organize. This will take time. This process has been tested by trial and error to save you time.

Day 1: Request Letters of Recommendation

You are going to be busy with the next steps for about two to three weeks. So, take advantage of this "busy work" time and ask for your letters of recommendation. This will give your teachers or professors enough time to write a good recommendation. Be sure to provide as many details about you, your goals, and your achievements as possible. These will be generic recommendation letters. Down the road, you may find that you may need to request letters of recommendation with very specific details. Have a list of several reliable resources, such as teachers, professors, counselors, etc. Do not use friends and acquaintances.

Day 2 to 4: Gather Information About YOU

Other than physical documents, all of the following will need to be in a word document so you can easily copy and paste. Scholarships will ask for this information over and over.

1. Copies of your latest official transcript. Will require an ink signature or stamp
2. Personal statement
3. Student resume
4. Student name, address, phone, email
5. Parent, name, address, phone, email
6. GPA
7. Rank, if in high school
8. College classes, if in high school
9. Advanced classes. High school and college
10. Volunteer work. Where, when, how many hours
11. Study abroad details
12. Academic awards
13. All other awards

14. Clubs

15. Memberships

16. Offices held

CAUTION, SCAM ALERT. DO NOT PROVIDE:

- Social security numbers

- Credit card numbers

- Tax documents

Day 5 to 10: Gather Your Resources

What are your resources? You will need catalogs of scholarships. There are several ways to obtain this information. Scholarship listing catalogs at a large bookstore, scholarship listing catalogs in the high school guidance counseling office, or college academic advising office, scholarship websites on the web, scholarships from your community college or university, local scholarships (in your place of residence), and my favorite… scholarships from the magic drawer. These are scholarships that your counselor has tucked away and are very hard to find.

If you order books online, it will take a few days for delivery. If you go to a large bookstore, you will need to take time to review books and make decisions for purchase. If you go to the counselor's office, you might need to make an appointment and make copies. This all takes time, but not much effort.

Pros and Cons of Each:

Catalog-Style Books from a Bookstore

Pros: you can thumb through the book and determine if the scholarship listing book is right for you before purchasing. All the information is laid out by categories. You will find categories of scholarships that you may not have realized were available. Most of the "secret scholarships" are listed. You can write in the book and make notes. There is no risk of scams, and it is a great investment. You know exactly what you are purchasing.

Cons: you must drive to the bookstore. Purchase required.

Books Online

Pros: convenient.

Cons: you can only rely on a short review. Inability to preview unless the online store has a lengthy preview section. You might order books that are not right for you.

Scholarships on the Web

Pros: convenient on your computer. Thousands of scholarships and tips. Utilize the most reputable sources. Many are free.

Cons: you will need to type in keywords for your needs. There may be categories that you did not know existed. You must input a lot of information to find out if the scholarship is for you. Could be a scam. Some require membership.

Scholarships at the Counselor's Office

Pros: you can make a copy from a scholarship book. Take extra coins so that you can make copies. Counselors have incredible knowledge of where to find money and usually have a secret stash.

Cons: you can't take their books home with you. You can't take the counselor home with you. You might need an appointment, and the appointment might not be long enough for your needs. You will have to drive to the office.

Day 6 to 10: The Search

Book Method: Allocate three to five nights to sit down and go through the scholarship listing books. Expect to spend one to two hours a night. No more than two hours, please. Do not attempt to do this in one sitting. Take your red pen and make notes and circle the ones that suit your needs and that you are qualified for. Highlight information. This is not the time to organize. This is the time to search. After you have searched, then we will organize. Do not take time to analyze. Just look for scholarships that you qualify for. You can do this independently or with your Dream Team, whichever suits you best.

Internet Method: Go to www.CollegeSurvivorBook.com in the University of Success section and view our recommended links. You will find reputable foundations and organizations that list thousands of scholarships. Now it will be up to you to enter the right search words and phrases. Then, you will need to go into the scholarship site and determine if it is right for you. You might have to pay a membership. Each site has a different navigation procedure. Expect to link out of the scholarship resource and go directly to the scholarship foundation, where you will have to register to find out if the scholarship is best for you.

Note:

There are pros and cons to the book method vs. the internet method. Our family prefers the book method as the start button. We found less than fifty scholarships on the internet, and it took a lot of time. We found 150 scholarships in the scholarship listing catalogs, and it took less time. Since we learned so much from the scholarship listing catalogs, we were able to enter new keywords into scholarship websites and find a few more scholarships that were not listed in the books. My best recommendation is to start with the scholarship listing catalog, then advance to the scholarship websites. Take advantage of all resources.

Day 11 to 21: Organizing

Take a few days' break from the search before beginning the organization.

The fastest way for you to organize your scholarship resources is to download our scholarship organizer spreadsheet from our website. This method is much faster than the paper method.

Ultimately, you will want to organize based on due date month. Let's demonstrate with the paper version. Visual learners will understand this, and conceptual learners will take this method to their computer and organize on virtual spreadsheets that are provided on our website. Available on www. CollegeSurvivorBook.com is a downloadable paper version and spreadsheet version. In addition, there is a video demonstration.

Paper Method:

1. Twelve three-ring binders (1 ½ inch)
2. One three-ring binder (1 inch)
3. Tabs (20 to 30), not dry erase version
4. Three-hole punch
5. Printer
6. Pencils and highlighters

Printer Tip:

Go to a large electronic retailer and ask for a printer with longevity. Toner will cost around $129 per year, and you should get 12,000 copies or more per toner. If you buy an inexpensive printer that requires cartridges, you will end up spending five to ten times more, plus gas, plus lost time going to the store to constantly buy cartridges. We learned the hard way. Be sure to print on greyscale or toner reduction mode or reduce the printing resolution to the lowest setting. Most settings offer 1200 DPI, 600DPI, and 300 DPI. Save your toner!

Why So Many Tabs?

These customized three-ring binders will last you for four years. You will be adding and deleting scholarship opportunities and updating information. And these catalogs may be passed on to siblings. Each and every scholarship has different rules and requirements, and this information should be organized so you can reference it easily. You are creating customized catalogs that will repeat each year. You only do the work once, then update the following years. Trust the process.

Your twelve binders will represent each month of the year. Keep in mind that you will begin applying for scholarships two months in advance of the actual due date. This means scholarships that are due in April will need your attention in February. Why? You may have to gather special letters of recommendation that are specific to the scholarship. You may have to write an essay along with a whole list of requirements. Give yourself plenty of time to get these things done. Our family learned the hard way—a life lesson we are passing on to you.

Binder Set-Up: Paper Method

1. 12 1 ½ inch binders will have 20 or more tabs and represent each month of the year.

2. Download and print the scholarship organizer worksheet from. www.CollegeSurvivorBook. com. The scholarship organizer worksheet will be inserted as the first page of each binder. Behind the first page of each binder will be the tabs. Behind each tab will be a copy of the scholarship you have applied for. You can make notes, highlight dates, etc. on these paper copies.

3. One one-inch binder. This binder will serve as your master file. This is where you manage your earnings. Download and print the"track my winnings" worksheet located at www. CollegeSurvivorBook.com in the University of Success section. This document is like a banking checkbook, so you can keep track of letters and checks and make sure that monies have arrived and have been applied correctly. This binder will also need tabs to track communication and problems. A video demonstration is available on www.CollegeSurvivorBook.com in the University of Success section.

Organizing: Paper Method

1. Start organizing the scholarships. It is easier to staple twelve scholarship organizer worksheets before beginning the process of organizing and documenting all your scholarship resources.

2. Only write in the name of the scholarship, due date, and the page number or source so you can find it. You do not need to add more information. Do not analyze. Do not overthink. Trust the process. Our family learned the hard way. We are teaching you the easy way. You are essentially making a list by month.

Ugh… how long is this going to take? I knew you would ask that. Time yourself, and you will get a good idea of your time commitment. It will seem like days, but it is just a few hours.

Online Support

On our website, there is a video demonstration available with extra tips and short cuts.

Tech Savvy: Spreadsheet Method

Follow the same directions. Your tabs are already formatted for you. Download your spreadsheet from our website. The spreadsheet method still takes time, but is so much faster than the paper method.

Cutting Corners

You can shorten your time and only look for scholarships under certain categories, such as ethnicity, race, state of residence, field of study, etc. but, you will have reduced the playing field by at least 50%. There are so many categories to choose from that the list seems endless. There are left-handed scholarships, red-headed scholarships, and take a selfie scholarships. There are contests and drawings. My best recommendation is to invest this time and discover all the potential so when you develop your plan, you will have a lot to choose from, and improve your chances of winning scholarships. Hindsight is 20/20.

Organized and Ready for the Next Step

How do you know you are ready? Well, once you have entered all the information from either your scholarship listing book or from the internet and can say, "I'm Done," then you are ready to move on to action, step 3.

Action, Step 3

There are three steps for the action section

1. First day of the month: decision

2. Dream Team

3. Brownie points

First Day of the Month: Decision

On the first day of each month, you will set aside one hour to look at the requirements of each scholarship for the due date month.

Example: This means that you are spending one hour on January 1st to decide which scholarships you will apply for with March due dates. You are spending one hour on Feb 1st to decide which scholarships you will apply for with April due dates, and so on. Because you did such a great job of organizing, all the information is right in front of you. You have a customized, cataloged list by month, so now you can go to each website and see what each opportunity requires, or if you used a book, you can refer to the page (much quicker). Then you pick the magic eight. Expect each month to provide numerous scholarship opportunities. It is almost impossible to apply for all of them. When our family first started this process, we thought that we could apply for each and every scholarship for the month. We learned the hard way, so we are teaching you the easier way. Our family recommends that you choose eight and realize that you might only apply for six.

Help with your decision process:

- ❖ Look at how many scholarships are being awarded by the foundation.
- ❖ How much is the scholarship worth?
- ❖ Is the scholarship program paying one big scholarship or fifty small scholarships?
- ❖ What are your best chances of winning?
- ❖ ·Do you need a special essay?
- ❖ Do you need a special letter of recommendation?

Reminder

You will apply for scholarships two months in advance of the due date. Why? You may have to gather letters of recommendation that are specific to the scholarship. You may have to write an essay along with a whole list of requirements. Give yourself plenty of time to get these things done.

Dream Team

Now you begin meeting with your Dream Team on a consistent basis. Even though you are working on your own scholarships, the team is there to provide support. Your CEO is keeping everyone on task, the communication specialist is keeping everyone aware of the latest news, the idea guru is providing ideas, and the analyst is there to help if you have computer problems. The perfect combination of a Dream Team. As you work together, time will pass very quickly. Your teammates will stumble upon scholarships that you did not know existed. Your team will run into problems, and together your team will find solutions. This is so much better than working alone. You will earn more money because of the team method, and momentum will be strong.

Brownie Points

Brownie points! Be sure to send a thank you note to the organization or foundation. Manners go a long way. Can you imagine a foundation receiving hundreds or thousands of entries for a scholarship and suddenly, a thank you note arrives in the mail? Simple curiosity will cause the person in charge to LOOK FOR YOU. It is very possible that the foundation may have your application in the top 20%, and that little thank you note will garner a tremendous amount of attention, all because of manners and a tribute to character. Something to think about! The squeaky wheel gets the grease. That grease might just mean that you are the winner of the scholarship!

Results and Repeat: Step 4

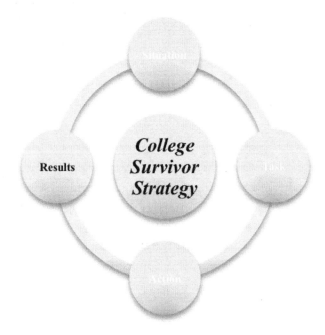

Let's say a few months have passed since your Dream Team started *College Survivor Strategy*. Hopefully, you should have received several award letters and checks.

As soon as letters and checks arrive, it is a good time to go back to your Financial Deficit Calculators and enter your new information. The Scholarship Deficit Calculator will provide new options based on the data that you enter. And the cycle will begin to repeat itself with new information. In fact, if anything changes—employment, financial aid, work-study etc…. you will need to enter new information.

If you are ahead of your goal of 20% successful applications, you could slow down your employment hours and reallocate your time to applying for more scholarships. If you are under the 20% goal, your team should help you figure out why. There could be a million reasons. A great team will be able to help you. Maybe your essays need work. Maybe you are applying for scholarships that have one winner and you are competing with thousands. Find your secret sauce. Research. But do not give up. Once you figure out your personal magic, you will continue to win and win.

Tracking My Winnings

Go to www.CollegeSurvivorBook.com in the University of Success Section and either print or download the Track My Winnings spreadsheet. This serves as your bank statement. The paper method will manage the paper version in the one-inch binder, and tech savvy will manage on the spreadsheet.

Every time you receive an award letter or check, enter in the information. Try not to say, "I'll do it later." This is your bank, and if you are receiving numerous awards, attention to detail is critical.

Analogy: If you were expecting a paycheck for $3,000, $5,000, and $10,000 and did not have a documentation process, then how would you know if the monies arrived and were applied appropriately?

Reflection

By now, you have digested a lot of information. You have determined your dreams and set your goals. You understand how *College Survivor Strategy* works to your advantage. You understand that the process takes time and that the first year is the hardest, but you also realize the payout. You also understand that the following years are much easier because you are organized and ready to go!

The effort and discipline with *College Survivor Strategy* is in your hands. The process is completely laid out in this book. You have access to www.CollegeSurvivorBook.com and the University of Success with teaching videos, demonstrations, documents, spreadsheets, calculators, and links to resources to help you. Everything is located in one spot so you will not have to spend endless hours looking and looking.

You can ask *College Survivor* questions and we will do our best to find you an answer. *College Survivor* is your HUB for so many categories of interest beyond scholarships and grants. If you are willing to learn, we are willing to teach!

Resources available at
www.CollegeSurvivorBook.com / University of Success section!
Remember! Believe in Yourself! You've Got This!

"I can remember college graduation day like it was yesterday. It was a hot August day, but it didn't matter. My anxious family sat patiently to hear my name. My heart was pounding. Now what?! My mind raced. No more finals. No more penny-pinching. A career waits! College was the best investment in my life."

P. Solis-Friederich, a new college graduate

CHAPTER 16
GRADUATION
WORDS OF WISDOM

"Hard work beats talent
when talent fails to work hard."
--Kevin Durant

In This Chapter

Words of wisdom from various mentors and life situations!

Mold Yourself

Take the best attribute of all those you encounter in your career and create a new you. Toss away the negative.

Eliminate Drama

This will deter advancement in your career.

Do Not Burn Bridges

No matter how wrong a situation or person may be toward you, turn the other cheek and be the better person. People are watching and listening. Burning bridges will haunt you later and could cost you your job or a reference for your next job. It is best to think about everything that could go wrong if you act in a rash manner. Sleep on it. Determine if the situation is a battle or a war. Then, make a decision by writing down the spin of your actions. Is it really worth it?

Manners

"Please" and "thank you" are the most respected. Manners are an indication of your character.

Create a Win-win Situation

No matter the profession, always make sure that all parties involved are winning. If the situation is one-sided, people take note and the ramification is that you will lose the respect of your peers and your supervisors or clients/customers.

Morals and Ethics

You may run into counterparts with low morals and ethics. Peer pressure rears its ugly head from the moment you start kindergarten all the way through your career, and even volunteer efforts. If you are uncomfortable with how a person in your circle of influence is exhibiting low morals and ethics, politely excuse yourself and stay away from adopting their methods.

Priorities

Keep your priorities in line: God (or your spiritual beliefs), family, work, everything else. If you mix up your priorities, you invite an unbalanced life.

Money

You will be rewarded for your efforts. As long as you are providing your employer with an amazing performance, the money will soon follow. On the other hand, if you know for certain that you are not paid appropriately for your service and you are unhappy, move on.

Happiness

If you are happy, that is awesome. If you are miserable, move on. Even if you need to take a pay cut to be happy, it is worth it. A miserable job can cause physical illness. Take care of yourself!

Practice Humility

No bragging. If your work is noteworthy, people will notice and may not say a word in front of you. They will talk when you are not around. Practicing humility earns you respect. It is better to have people say good things about you behind your back than bad things in front of you.

Treat All With Kindness:

Today's mailroom guy could be your future boss! I have a personal friend that started in the mailroom and fifteen years later was the vice president of the company. In addition, treating those who might not have an opportunity for advancement can positively impact your career. For example, the janitor who takes out your office trash and wipes your desk every night deserves a thank-you card. Can you imagine how that would make him feel? Trust me, good things come to those who give. Do random acts of kindness. That janitor may just find an important document in the trash and think to place it back on your desk and save your career. You never know.

Resources available at
www.CollegeSurvivorBook.com / University of Success section!
Remember! Believe in Yourself! You've Got This!

"I can remember as if it were yesterday… I moved to Bryan, Texas to begin my college years at Texas A&M University. A week later, my dear favorite Uncle Robert came to visit. He brought me tools. I still have that hammer. You need tools to execute your plan."

P. Solis-Friederich, the college student armed with tools

CHAPTER 17
UNIVERSITY OF SUCCESS
ONLINE RESOURCES

"Using all of your resources wisely is the key for growth, which opens up success. Unfortunately, most do not realize this, and the door of opportunity stays closed."
--Lincoln Patz

In This Chapter

1. Documents

2. Checklists

3. Questions (Academic / Financial)

4. Academic Tips

5. Single Parents

6. Calculators

7. Worksheets

University of Success is available in our website, www.CollegeSurvivorBook.com. University of Success is designed to help you—the parent and the student. University of Success is an extension of the *College Survivor* book. The purpose is to save you time and effort. Numerous areas of resources have been researched, organized and are available for you. Most resources are downloadable and printable for your use. As mentioned earlier in the book, our family is in a ten to twelve-year college learning curve. Resources are updated frequently to give you the most accurate information in one user-friendly area. Essentially, we have done the work for you! University of Success is your one-stop shop of documents, checklists, tips, and most importantly—calculators, to save you hours and hours of mathematical processing.

Documents

Parent/Student Commitment Contract – page 173

(Chapter 9, 10, 14, 15, 17)

A document for parents and students with the purpose of commitment to subsidizing specific expenses.

What If – Role Play – page 192

(Chapter 9, 10, 14, 15, 17)

A document for mentors and students or a college Dream Team. This is a role-play document that places the college student in a problem situation. These problems are real and happen every day.

Scams/Identity Theft Alert – page 174

(Chapter 9, 10, 14, 15, 17)

A document that provides information about fraud prevention and solutions.

Roommate Contract Terms– page 176

(Chapter 7, 9, 10, 11, 12, 17)

A document that provides a list of critical items for discussion with a new roommate. You can design your own contract or utilize our provided links to preformatted roommate agreement contracts.

Roommate Conflict Resolution Strategy – page 177

(Chapter 7, 9, 10, 11, 12, 17)

A document that provides solutions to problems with roommates

Checklists

Off to College (Dorm) – page 179

(Chapter 9, 10, 17)

Off to College (First Apartment) – page 180

(Chapter 9, 10, 17)

These documents are packing checklists.

Questions (Academic / Financial)

List of questions – High School Guidance Counselor – page 181

(Chapter 9, 10, 12, 17)

List of questions – College Financial Aid Advisor – page 182

(Chapter 9, 10, 12, 17)

These lists of questions are designed for parents and students to ask counselors and advisors.

Academic Tips

Power of the Transcript (High School) – page 184

(Chapter 2, 9, 10, 12, 17)

Final Exam Preparation (College) – page 186

(Chapter 9, 10, 12, 17)

Low GPA Strategy (High School and College) – page 190

(Chapter 2, 9, 10, 12, 17)

These documents provide tips for academic strategy.

Single Parents – You've Got This! – page 195.

(Chapter 7, 5, 12, 15, 17)

Advice and strategy for single parents in college.

Calculators

The *College Survivor* calculators are developed to support *College Survivor Strategy*. Some of the calculators are downloadable and some are not. As for the non-downloadable calculators, the information that you enter and your results will be automatically emailed to you for your records or you can print the results. These calculators are invaluable in executing your *College Survivor Strategy*. They will save you time and energy and provide an up-to-date plan in seconds. All calculators are available at www.collegesurvivorbook.com in the University of Success section.

Savings in a Jar Calculator (downloadable)

Parents, grandparents

(Chapter 4, 17)

This is a simple calculator that can provide an estimate of saving any dollar amount for any specific period of time.

Budget Calculator (link provided)

Parents, high school students, college students

(Chapter 3, 4, 6, 7, 9, 17)

The University of Success provides links to the best budgeting calculators available online. There are hundreds to choose from. You can select the budgeting calculator that suits your needs or research for a different budgeting calculator. The resources online are incredible.

Employment Calculator: High School Student Wage Projection (downloadable)

Parents, high school students, college students

(Chapter 4, 9, 15, 17)

This calculator will assist the high school student in developing a plan for working and saving in high school by the month and the year. An estimated final total will be provided for the remaining high school months and years prior to college. Use this calculator over and over with a wage increase or hour increase or decrease. The calculator follows *College Survivor Strategy* and assists with a savings plan.

Employment Calculator: College Student Wage Projection (downloadable)

Parents, high school students, college students

(Chapter 15, 17)

This calculator will assist the college student in developing a plan for saving by the month and the year while in college. An estimated final total will be provided for the remaining college months and years. Use this calculator over and over with a wage increase or hour increase or decrease. The calculator follows *College Survivor Strategy* and assists with a savings plan.

UNIVERSITY OF SUCCESS : ONLINE RESOURCES

Financial Deficit Calculator (not downloadable)

Parent/Mentor, high school students, college students

(Chapter 3, 4, 15, 17)

This calculator will determine your financial deficit (gap) for the future or remaining months of high school and college. This calculator is necessary for *College Survivor Strategy*. Your results will be emailed to you. Use this calculator over and over when there is a change in wage or addition of financial aid or scholarships. This calculator does not provide options to close the gap. It only provides your financial gap and is for informational purposes.

Scholarship Deficit Calculator (not downloadable)

Parent/mentor, high school students, college students

(Chapter 15, 17)

This calculator will implement your financial deficit (gap) in conjunction with the future or remaining months of high school plus college and provide several options for closing the financial gap. This calculator should be used monthly to provide a sound financial plan. This calculator is necessary for *College Survivor Strategy*. Your results will be emailed to you. It is up to you to decide which option is best for your unique situation so that you will have a plan to close your financial gap and graduate as debt-free as possible. Refer to Chapter 3, Tony and Tina, scenario #4.

Example of Scholarship Deficit Calculator results:

- ❖ Dream Team meetings: recommended times per month/year.
- ❖ Dream Team hours per meeting: recommended hours per meeting by month/year.
- ❖ Scholarship applications: recommended dollars and hours per month/year.
- ❖ Smart poor: recommended reduction in living costs by month/week/day.
- ❖ Projected loans: estimated loans per year if the above recommendations are not achievable.

Worksheets

Scholarship Organizer Worksheet (downloadable)

Parents, grandparents, high school students, college students

(Chapter 15, 17)

Necessary to organize scholarship information in order to execute *College Survivor Strategy*

Track My Winnings Worksheet (downloadable)

Parents, grandparents, high school students, college students

(Chapter 15, 17)

A worksheet designed to track your winnings. Essentially a bank statement.

Resources available at
www.CollegeSurvivorBook.com / University of Success section!
Remember! Believe in Yourself! You've Got This!

Parent/Student Commitment Contract

I_____ (your mentor and support) will commit to the following items for your support. Ex: insurance, groceries, gas, portion of living, books, etc.)	I_____ (student) will commit to subsidizing following items. Ex: insurance, groceries, gas, portion of living, books, etc.)
1	1
2	2
3	3
4	4
5	5
6	6
7	7
8	8
9	9
10	10
Specific Details:	Specific Details:
Date	Date
Signature	Signature

Scams/Identity Theft Alert

Caller ID

If someone calls asking for money or personal information such as your bank account or social security number, hang up. If you think the caller might be telling the truth, call back to a number you know is genuine or ask them for their name and number. They will hang up if they are a scammer.

Paying for a promise

You may be asked for advance payment for debt relief, loans, or a job. They might even say you've won a prize. Hang up!

How you pay

Credit cards have fraud protection, but some payment methods don't. Wiring money through services like Western Union or MoneyGram is risky because it's impossible to get your money back. The same is true for reloadable cards. Note: Government offices and reputable companies won't require you to use these payment methods.

Robocalls

If you answer the phone and hear a recorded sales pitch, hang up. If you stay on the line, you risk the caller retaining more information from you that could lead to more calls.

FAFSA is free

If you are asked for money, it is a scam.

Free trial offers

Some companies use free trials to sign you up for products and bill you every month until you cancel. And they make it almost impossible to cancel. Research the company and read the cancellation policy. Be sure to check your bank statement every month for charges that you did not approve.

Fake checks

By law, banks must make funds from deposited checks available within days but uncovering a fake check can take weeks. You will be responsible for repaying the bank if the check is fake.

Scam alerts

Sign up for alerts from the FTC at ftc.gov/scams. This will come straight to your email.

Search online

Type in the suspicious company name, then negative words like complaint, review, negative, scam, IRS, legal, lawsuit and see what you find. Seek, and you shall find.

Report identity theft

Take immediate action! Act quickly. Contact one of the following offices; you will get help.

- ❖ U.S. Department of Education Office of Inspector General Fraud Hotline
- ❖ Federal Trade Commission
- ❖ Social Security Administration
- ❖ Equifax Credit Bureau
- ❖ Experian Information Solutions
- ❖ TransUnion Credit Bureau

Report Financial Aid Fraud

If a company charges for financial aid advice and does not deliver what it promises, the company may be fraudulent. Contact the Federal Trade Commission and the Consumer Financial Protection Bureau.

Roommate Contract Terms

There are numerous versions online, or you can create your own. This is a complete list of items that should be in your roommate agreement. Look for links to several roommate agreement documents on www.CollegeSurvivorBook.com

Roommate agreement should include:

1. **Rental/Lease Agreement** (list start and end date of agreement):

2. **Rent shall be payable on the** _____ day of each month. Late fees apply to those who are late.

3. **Security Deposit.** The total security deposit for the unit is $_____. Each Roommate will pay their portion. Each Roommate will receive a his/her share of the deposit when the landlord returns it at the end of the tenancy (including deductions).

4. **Living Arrangements.** The bedroom(s) will be allocated as follows:

5. **Special "house rules"** about sharing space, furniture, appliances, and food in the apartment are:

6. **Overnight Guests Rules**:

7. **Utility and Telephone Charges**:

8. **Household Chores Per Person**:

9. **Cleanliness Expectations**:

10. **Pets**:

11. **Noise Level**:

12. **Alcohol and Smoking**:

13. **Parking**:

14. **Additional Remarks**:

15. **Roommate Move Out Procedure**:

16. **New Roommate Move in Procedure**:

17. **Consequences of Breaking the Agreement**:

18. **Roommate Signatures and Date**:

Roommate Conflict Resolution Strategy

Here come Dr. Jekyll and Mr. Hyde. Your friend may be the life of the party and so much fun! But living with them could be joyous, or your worst nightmare. You might want to get in touch with their former roommate and find out what life was like. Also, find out why this person needs a new roommate. Maybe they did not pay their bills or were evicted—red flag! Keep an open mind and be prepared for someone who might do and think differently from you. Learning to live with someone is one of the steps of preparing for adulthood. Learning to get along with all types of people has been part of your life since the day you were born, and it will continue. Wait until you meet Mr. / Mrs. Grouchy Pants, your friendly and not-so-friendly boss at your first professional job.

Finding the Win-Win Situation

Communication is key in building strong roommate relationships. It is encouraged to complete a roommate agreement. Dealing with conflict early will promote stronger relationships and decrease frustration. You will already have enough on your plate. Conflict does not need to be added.

Plan Ahead

If you're an incoming student, you are probably pretty nervous about the roommate situation. You might even decide to find a roommate ahead of time. Instead, perhaps your college has a pairing program that finds the best roommate for you based on academic major, hobbies, personality, etc.

Useful Tips on Handling Conflict

1. Acknowledge your differences and similarities. Laugh about it!

2. Create some ground rules.

3. Develop a living plan that you can agree upon.

4. Stay away from discussing politics and religion. This is a mixture for disaster.

5. Devise a conflict resolution plan. Example: If we have a conflict or disagreement, we will resolve it this way:_____.

6. Still can't resolve the problem? If you are in the dorm, your resident assistant can help you. If you are in an apartment, bring in an unbiased party to mitigate. The conflict could be large or small. Either way, an unbiased person can really help, and save a friendship.

7.   No way out? Move on and move out. It is not worth the stress.

8.   DO NOT PAY YOUR ROOMATE'S RENT! If you do, you can expect to pay it again!

Off to College – Dorm

Office/ Electronics	Office/ Electronics	Linens/Laundry Supplies	Clothes/ Toiletries	Room/ Storage	Medical
3x5 Index cards Backpack Binder clips Binders Bulletin board Desk lamp Dry erase board Dry erase markers Flash drives Folders Mini tool kit Notebooks Paperclips Pencil holder Pencil sharpener Pens and pencils Push pins Storage bins Trash can TV and DVD player	Audio Equipment Backpack Cell charger Cell phone Desk trays Ear plugs Electronics Envelopes Extension cords Extra tape Headphones Laptop Paper for printer Portable speakers Printer Rubber bands Rulers Scissors Stamps Stapler Sticky notes Surge suppressor Tape dispenser	Blankets Comforter Detergent Drying rack Laundry basket Linens Mesh zipper bag for delicates Pillow Quarters Shams Sheets Softener Stain remover Towels Washcloth	Clothes Comb/brush Conditioner Cotton swabs Dental floss Facial products Hair dryer Hair products Hair tools Hangers Lint brush Lotion Nail clippers Razor Shampoo Shoes Shower caddy Shower shoes Soap Socks Swimsuit Toothbrush Toothpaste Tweezers Undergarments	Art Bins Bowls Coffee maker Cups Glasses Dish soap Extra key Fan Food storage Hot pot Lightbulbs Microwave Mini refrigerator Paper towels Picture hangers Plates Posters Rug Safe for valuables Tissues Umbrella Under bed storage Utensils Wash rag Water bottle	Antacid Antidiarrheal medicine Cough drops Feminine supplies First aid kit Pain relief Meds Vitamins Wet wipes Car Tire Gauge Emergency Kit Flat tire compressor Winter Emergency Kit Extra Windshield Fluid Extra Oil Funnel for oil Extra key

Off to College – First Apartment

Kitchen	Bathroom	Bedroom	Living Room	Laundry	Home Improvement/ Misc.
Aluminum foil Blender Bottle opener Broom Can opener Coffeemaker Colander Cutlery Dish drying rack Dish soap Dish towels Dishes and bowls Duster Dustpan Garbage bags Hand soap Knife set Meat thermometer Microwave Mugs Oven mitts Paper towels Plastic wrap Pots and pans Serving dishes Serving utensils Slotted spoons Slow cooker Sponges Standing mixer Swiffer Toaster and/or toaster oven Tupperware Wastepaper basket Water pitcher/filter Wooden spoons	Air freshener Bath mat Bath towels Cleaning supplies Hand towels Rug Scale Shower curtain Shower organizers Toilet paper Toilet plunger Toiletries	Alarm clock Bed Closet organizers Comforter Curtains or blinds Desk and chair Dressers End table or nightstand Full-length mirror Hangers Jewelry box or stand/organizer Over-the-door storage units Safe Several sets of sheets Shoe rack Storage boxes Under-the-bed box	Area rug Chairs Coffee table Couch Curtains or blinds Floor lamp Ottoman Throw blankets Throw pillows TV stand	Drying rack Garment bag Hamper and/or laundry bags Iron Ironing board Lingerie bag/mesh wash bags	Adhesive hooks Basic tools such as a screwdriver and hammer Batteries Bookcases Carbon monoxide detector Doormat Emergency/First Aid kit Extension cords Fan or air conditioner Flashlight for emergencies Nails Shelving Surge protectors

LIST OF QUESTIONS
High School Guidance Counselor

GPA

How often are my grades evaluated? Every quarter, trimester, semester? Is my GPA weighted? Example: Are accelerated classes worth more?

Classes

Which classes are included in my GPA? Only completed, dropped, incomplete?

Ranking

How does the ranking system work? Example: #45 out of 150 is the same as top 30%.

Extra-Curricular

Is my profile included? Example: Attendance, community service, list of honors, and advanced placement classes.

Tips

❖ Request a copy of your high school transcript so you can review for accuracy.

❖ Know the differences between cumulative GPA and non-cumulative GPA. Colleges look at both, but are most concerned with the cumulative GPA.

❖ Investigate the average GPA for the college you want to attend. Have a choice of five to ten colleges so you will have a plan B in the event that your #1 choice of college requires a GPA that is higher than yours.

❖ If you have dreams of going to college and your GPA is slowing you down, find a way and never give up.

❖ It is highly recommended to add your student resume to your application. Counselors like seeing a well-rounded student.

LIST OF QUESTIONS
College Financial Aid Advisor

If the administrator cannot answer your questions or says "sign here," do not sign until you get an explanation and fully understand the small print.

Special Financial Programs

Does your institution have a program to meet my financial need after I receive my financial award letter? (This is the gap)

Reduction of Financial Aid Because of Scholarships

If I receive scholarships, will my need-based financial package be reduced?

Reduction of Financial Aid Because of Grants

If I receive a scholarship, will this affect any grants that I may have been awarded?

Grant Opportunities

Do you have grants available through your institution? Can I apply?

Scholarship Opportunities

Do you have scholarships available through your institution? Can I apply? Are they renewable?

Application of Award Monies

How are funds applied? (Example: 1st grants, 2nd financial aid, 3rd scholarships.)

Increase in College Costs

How much have your college's costs increased in the last three years?

Fees

What additional fees can I expect? Parking, food, major-related expenses?

Debt:

What percentage of students graduate with debt and what is the average cumulative debt at graduation?

Eligibility Requirements

Are there rules for keeping my grants and scholarships in future years? GPA? Enrollment status? Special activities? Community service?

Residency Requirements

Am I required to live in the dorm? If yes, how long?

Work-Study Questions

How much will I be paid per hour? Are student employment opportunities difficult and why? Are there jobs related to my academic major? Am I guaranteed a job? What types of jobs are available? How will I be paid—check, direct deposit, applied to my bill? Pay frequency?

Financial Aid Appeal

How do I appeal my award letter if my family's financial circumstances have changed or will change?

Law Changes

Are there any laws that will impact my award next year and the following years?

Too much scholarship money

What happens if I receive too many scholarships and the money is sent to your institution and shows a positive balance? What happens to the money? What about taxes?

Power of the Transcript
High School

The Transcript

Admissions counselors look at your transcript in several different ways. The overall GPA is an indication of how hard you worked over the course of your academic years. Class rank is important for some colleges, but not for all. Counselors consider the areas in which you excel and how it relates to the major or type of degree that you have chosen. This is a very important part of your application process. However, this is one component of your college application. Extra-curricular and volunteer work are also taken into consideration at some colleges, but not all. Some colleges look at the overall GPA and make their decision of admission.

What Impresses an Administrator?

The class selection. Did you take advanced placement classes? Did you take online college courses while in high school?

What Does Not Impress an Administrator?

A class selection of non-academic classes. Although you may have excellent grades in classes that are not as challenging, administrators are looking for students who are serious about planning for college and have taken the time to prepare for college courses.

GPA and Class Rank

Some schools only consider core classes (English, Math, Science, and Social Studies) when calculating your GPA. Other schools examine grades for all your classes. Each college is different.

GPA Consistency

A consistent GPA is golden. These are the cream-of-the-crop candidates. They are willing to work hard, and they enjoy challenging themselves to learn new things while maintaining a high GPA.

GPA Improvement

Students that had a rough start but then skyrocketed in subsequent years show the counselor that something changed. Counselors also look for this situation because it shows maturity and dedication to pursuing college, even though it is indicated later in the life of the transcript. The student will have an opportunity to provide information about this change in GPA and explain the change. The reason could be anything: family tragedy, medical emergency or even maturity. Ultimately, counselors are looking for character and dedication to pursuing a higher education.

Pass/Fail Classes

Try to avoid these classes. They are often considered D classes in the eyes of counselors at some colleges.

Behavior Record

If you were never suspended, you will have nothing to worry about. If you have been suspended, counselors will not be impressed. This does not mean that you are banned from college. This just means that you may have to prove your character via a community college or trade school to avoid the negative impact of a behavior report.

Strategy

Every college is different. Every counselor is different. Find out what they are looking for in a transcript and give them what they want. If you are in a tough situation with your GPA, write a letter of explanation or make an appointment in person (if it is allowed). The worst-case scenario is that you may attend a college that is not your first choice, prove that you are worthy with stellar grades, then transfer. This is actually a great strategy. Transfer students with stellar grades can receive more scholarships because of the new start. Starting over after high school provides a clean slate. This may be your best strategy.

Final Exam Preparation
College

Dream Team

The team does not meet two weeks before exams.

Eliminate distractions

When studying, eliminate chatty friends, social media, turn off your phone (vibrate does not count). Make sure that the social media alerts are not turned on your laptop. Find a secret place to study.

Time Block Management

Your study schedule should be divided into small units of time. Take breaks. Do not wait till you feel like studying. Commit to the time block that you scheduled. If you have committed to studying for English from 2:00 P.M. to 4:00 P.M. on Wednesday, then stay with the plan.

Not a Time to Party

Celebrate when finals are over.

Procrastination is Not Your Friend

It is recommended to schedule two weeks to study, not the night before.

Assuming You Know It:

This will bite you every time. Over-study!

Reduce Employment Hours

Although *College Survivor Strategy* says to work twenty-four hours per week during the academic year, you will need to reduce the two weeks before finals and make up the hours after finals or earlier in the semester.

Know the Format of the Exam

Is the exam multiple choice or do you have to write an essay? This will impact how you study.

Review

Review old tests, study guides, or the course objectives.

Organize a Study Group

It is very likely that someone in the study group may teach you something that you did not know or understand.

Misunderstanding

If you are struggling with a section, ask your professor or a friend from the class that does well.

Get a tutor

The best time to ask for a tutor is at the beginning of the semester. You will know if you need extra help. It is ok to ask for help.

Develop summary sheets

Your class notes should be in summary form for each class.

Check the internet for study aids

There are numerous sources available online that may be related to the course book that you bought.

Make sure your goals are realistic

Set realistic goals or you will become overwhelmed.

Can't remember certain formulas or main ideas?

Many students will create a rhyme, song, saying or funny acronym.

Time yourself

A great strategy is 45 minutes of study and a 15-minute break. Repeat.

Sleep when it is time

Go to bed early and rise early. Getting proper rest will help your memory.

Procrastination

Final Exam time is not the best time to binge-watch a show.

Energy drinks

The crash will not be good.

Say it

Teach yourself out loud. You will be amazed how much you retain by verbalizing information.

Look for illustrations and graphics

Illustrations and graphs or graphics located in your book can help you identify the message. This will help with conceptual learning.

Investigate

Find out what the professor likes to read in an essay and give the professor exactly what they are looking for.

Quiz yourself

Cover up your notes and try to explain them to yourself or a study buddy.

Flashcards

Flashcards take time to make. There are several online programs where you can enter the information and learn from the flashcards in the virtual world. These sites also keep track of your score. You should start this at the beginning of the semester so you are not taking a tremendous amount of time entering information. Some sites have games with the information.

Anxiety

Anxiety is not your friend. If you wait till the last minute to study, expect anxiety to visit. If anxiety is a problem, use your search engine to find coping skills or talk it out with a friend.

Nutrition

There are numerous sites that give a list of brain food. Your choices will impact your mental energy. The best brain food before a test is fish, greens, and blueberries.

Check the 5 best strategies for you.

Commit.

Plan the work, work the plan.

Low GPA Strategy

High School and College

Life is not over because of grades. Every student has an opportunity for an education, just in different ways. Dreams can still turn into goals, and goals into plans. A higher GPA is better, but a lower GPA does not mean a student is not allowed to get an education. In so many cases, there have been students with incredible potential and intelligence but with a less-than-stellar GPA. Self-motivation, boredom, home environment—anything can impact a GPA. The most important thing is that the student wants to go to college. If they do not want to go to college, then failure is not too far off. Students must follow their own dreams, not the dreams of others.

Self-evaluation

What are the dreams of this student? Then, how can the dreams turn into goals? Does this student require a formal education or trade school? Then form the plan.

Start at a Community College

After community college, transfer to the university of your choice. Maturity may be the factor. Many students will have poor grades in high school and then stellar grades in college. When transferring, the admissions office will take this into consideration.

Take Responsibility

Be honest and forthright with the admissions office. Provide a letter of explanation. Anything could have impacted the grades—family tragedy, medical issues, divorce, maturity, etc.

Character

A letter of recommendation from teachers and counselors can go a long way. Reach out to teachers for help.

Wait

Apply during regular admission. All the early admissions may be filled, but there still may be spots to fill. This way, you are not competing with the early applicants. This is not a guarantee of acceptance, but a very good strategy that does work.

Parents, college is not for every child. Some love to work. And that is okay. The best thing you can do is talk about it and support your child's decision. Time will pass, and they will become adults. There are many adults that return to school on their terms. This could be your child. But if your child does want to go to college, a less-than-stellar GPA does not mean that they are not allowed in college. This is simply not true. They can attend a community college. There are other options, such as trade school. And it is possible that your child is so undecided that they are frustrated. Perhaps they have anxiety because they do not know what they want to do when they grow up. A counselor can assist with this, and test for potential career choices. Support and give the best guidance possible and know you have done your best.

What If?

How Does it Work?

The mentor (parent or older fellow student) should ask the question and the new or future student(s) should answer the question.

The role of the mentor is to coach and guide the student(s) to the best solution, not answer the question outright. After asking and solving each problem, ask the following questions.

1. Does your answer solve the situation?
2. Could you have prevented the situation?
3. Now that you have solved the problem, what is your plan B in case it happens again?
4. What did we learn from this situation?
5. Do you have any questions?
6. Can you handle this on your own?

SITUATION: you worked all summer and you are settling in. You have saved $3000. You are moving into your new apartment with your best friend. What expenses do you expect? How much do you think they will cost?

SITUATION: everything is going great, then your roommate has an unexpected family emergency and has to move home. They are unable to pay their half of the living expenses. What do you do? What is your plan B?

SITUATION: a person runs into your car and leaves the scene. Your car is completely totaled. What do you do? Now you do not have transportation!

SITUATION: you caught the flu and do not work for seven days. You have missed class and work. What do you do?

SITUATION: you accidentally tap a car while trying to park. No one is looking. You do not see any damage. What do you do?

SITUATION: you go to a party and as you are going to the bathroom, you see a door open with students doing drugs. What do you do?

SITUATION: you have lost your wallet and check your bank to find that someone stole your identity and your money. What do you do?

SITUATION: you go out with friends. After the party, the driver is drunk and will not give away the keys. What do you do?

SITUATION: you go out with friends and they decide to pull a prank on you. They drop you off in the middle of the country and take your phone. What do you do?

SITUATION: your car breaks down in the middle of traffic. There is traffic everywhere and it is dangerous to get out of your car. Your phone is dead. What do you do?

SITUATION: you accidentally left your apartment or dorm room unlocked. When you return, your computer is gone. What do you do?

SITUATION: you get a flat tire with a dead phone and no road side assistance to help you. What do you do?

SITUATION: you run out of gas on a road with very few cars. Your phone is dead. What do you do?

SITUATION: you wake up with 102-degree fever and think you have the flu. It is finals time. You have to take two finals today, one tomorrow and three the next day. What do you do?

SITUATION: your roommate has a habit of wearing your clothes without asking. What do you do?

SITUATION: your roommate asks to borrow money. What do you do?

SITUATION: during a test, the person sitting next to you continually looks at your answers and you are quite certain that they are cheating. What do you do?

SITUATION: your professor returns your research paper and you receive a less than stellar grade. This is the first time that you have ever received a less than stellar grade. What do you do?

SITUATION: you return to your apartment after work and find your roommate engaged in drug use. What do you do?

SITUATION: you are walking to your car after an evening class and a suspicious person is following you to your car. What do you do?

SITUATION: your best friend tells you about criminal activity that they were involved in. What do you do?

SITUATION: your best friend is in dire straits due to an incident. They need you to comfort them but, the timing is difficult. It is finals time and you need to study. What do you do?

Single Parents: You've Got This!

Dear Single Parents,

I have been in your shoes. You can do this. There are so many resources for you. Use your search engine to find help. *College Survivor Strategy* is your missing link. You should meet with a Dream Team of single parents every week, except the two weeks before finals. Stay on course, and you should have enough in scholarships, grants, and financial aid to either reduce your employment load or completely eliminate employment. Then, you can focus on study and family. If you have small children, your Dream Team can take turns babysitting so the other team members can study. If you have teenagers, give them a grocery budget and have them shop. Take turns making meals and have a chore schedule. You are not the servant!

Time management is critical in your life. Small increments of time will reduce your stress and anxiety. Utilize apps to remember everything for you. Take that strain off your brain. Follow *College Survivor Strategy*. Plan the work, work the plan. Graduate! Your children will be watching and learning from your discipline, and they will want to be like you. What a gift you are providing your family. Hang in there. You've got this!

Your Support Network

You will need more than your Dream Team. If you have small children, can your parents or close friends babysit to give you extra time? If your children are teenagers, go hide in the library. Have a plan, and don't feel guilty. Write thank you notes to those who help you. Leave love notes for your kids. Review: The Dream Team, chapter 13, page 111.

Child Care

Perhaps the school has a program for child care. Ask. In addition, you will have to find care centers that exist beyond working hours. Negotiate a price. Volunteer for free care. There are ways to get around child care.

Time Block Management:

College Survivor Strategy teaches time block management in the book and on www.CollegeSurvivorBook.com. Time management is an art. Master time, and you will be less stressed. Your secret sauce is staying on task, not veering from the plan, and running a tight ship at your house. Consistent homework time, chore time, and bed time for your family is highly recommended. Review : Time Block Management, Chapter 12, page 106.

Balance

If you are unbalanced, you will be overwhelmed. Review: Chapter 12, page 98.

Professors Will Listen

Talk to your professor and let them know you are a single parent, especially if you have small children. Children get sick and need you. Have a plan to get notes if you miss a class. Have a plan in the event that you miss a test. Communication is key!

Family Time

Your children will have homework too. Do it together. Considering the fact that you are on the go, this may be your only time for family time. No matter the age of your child or children, sitting together and working together will create a bond. And remember, they are watching your actions and will want to be like you someday.

No Time for Guilt

Emotions are like visitors. They come to visit, then leave. Sometimes visitors overstay their welcome, and you have to politely ask them to leave. If guilt is an unwanted visitor, politely ask it to leave. Show guilt the door and say to it, "Don't let the door hit your behind on the way out!"

Take Care of Yourself

That means nutrition, hydration, and time for yourself. If you are having problems with balance, then review Chapter 12, page 98.

(Summer 1986) Phyllis Solis, Age 20, single parent sophomore in college

Statement of Purpose

Mission Statement

"Our mission is to successfully coach students and parents how to transform their dreams and goals into a reality, one day, one scholarship, and one happy student at a time."

Vision Statement

"Our vision is to be a household name for generations to come, by providing quality products, quality customer service, and rewarding students for their excellence."

Philosophy

"Our first priority is inspiring and coaching individuals to higher education."

Rule of Thumb

"Always learn from all generations. Mentor the next generation as if they were the last."

Giving Back

We are a blessed family. There comes a time when a life event changes your entire perspective. That day came on a beautiful sunny day in July 2001 with the birth of our youngest child. From his first breath, he was a fighter: a gorgeous baby boy with one issue of the heart. He was born with transposition of the greater vessels and required immediate surgery. I can remember sitting in my hospital room and hearing babies cry to the left and right, and I did not have a crying baby. He gently lay in his tiny bed in the NICU. On the fifth day of his life, I was able to hold him for maybe five minutes. It seemed like thirty seconds. Then, the nurse took him to surgery. Our world changed. Our life changed. Our view of life's little things changed. We changed, forever. Our two-year-old daughter was a breath of fresh air and provided much needed therapy for the soul.

Almost seventeen years later, and a total of four surgeries to date, we have the most amazing young man. I thank the Lord for this miracle. I am a better person because of that sunny day in July. I see everything in a different light.

So, we give back and ask nothing in return. Every book, product, or service that is sold under the *College Survivor* name contributes to several charity organizations. They are listed on our website. It is the right thing to do, and that is why we do it. I have learned that sometimes we cannot understand why. I realize now that it is not our job to understand why.

I have learned that each of us have our own personal book collection with volumes and chapters. And it is our job to live life to the fullest so that this book collection can be written. We are not provided the privilege of skipping to the last chapter to see how it ends. We must have faith that the story will have several plots and twists and turns to make the story very interesting. Without skipping to the last chapter and just having faith, I am certain that a great ending awaits.

> "God is using your present circumstances
> to make you more useful
> for later roles in his unfolding story."
> --Louie Giglio

Priorities in Life

#1 God

#2 Family

#3 Work

#4 Everything Else

Our son, W. Friederich, showing off his purple-painted finger nails, painted by a little girl with cancer at his favorite camp for heart and cancer kiddos. June 2017.

W. Friederich returns from his annual camp for children with congenital heart issues and childhood cancer. The camp is located at Shepherd's Fold Ranch located in Avant, Oklahoma and sponsored by The Children's Hospital at Saint Francis, Tulsa, Oklahoma. W. Friederich will start his first year as a fore runner in summer 2018. This is the precursor to becoming a camp counselor. W. Friederich has been attending since he was eight years old and wants to become a full time counselor in the future. He intends to attend college and graduate with a bachelor's degree in Education/History.

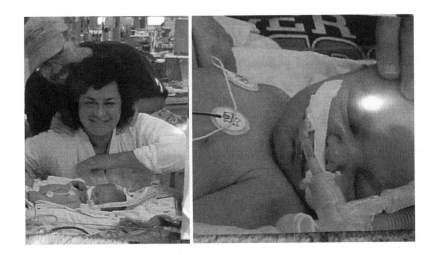

Our son, W. Friederich in the Neonatal Intensive Care Unit, Saint Francis Hospital, Tulsa, Oklahoma. He was only hours old, waiting for his first open heart surgery at age 5 days, July 2001.

My parents, Mr. and Mrs. Solis, Oct 2014. Our daughter, M. Friederich, Dec 2017.

Top: (left to rIght)

K. and P. Friederich with W. Friederich in the NICU, Saint Francis Hospital, Tulsa, Oklahoma, July 2001.

W. Friederich, in the NICU, Saint Francis Hospital, Tulsa, Oklahoma, July 2001.

Bottom: (left to right)

Mr. R. F. Solis, B.A., M.S., Education. high school band director, choral director, high school Spanish teacher. Teacher for over 40 years. During his career, he spoke five languages, played 14 instruments, and painted like Picasso.

Mrs. M.P. Solis, B.A. Education, Texas Women's University. Elementary and Special Education teacher for 20 years.

Miss M. Friederich, college-bound, fall 2018. Bio Chemistry / Pre-Med.

The two Mrs. Friederichs, Aug 2017.   The two Mr. Friederichs, Aug 2017.

Left to right:

Mrs. P. Friederich, B.A., Speech Communications, Texas A&M University. Corporate career, business owner, substitute teacher, author of College Survivor.

Mrs. P. Friederich, B.A., Education, Southern State Teacher's College. Kindergarten and art teacher. Teacher for 43 years, author and illustator of Storytime: Once Upon A Time, Volume I & 2.

Mr. K. Friederich, B.S. Economics and Business Development, University of South Dakota. Business analyst, business owner.

Mr. L. Friederich, School of Hard Knocks. Grocery store owner for 30 years. Refrigeration and appliance business owner for 20 years.

How the Name *"College Survivor"* was born...

When I was in the process of writing the original workshop in 2016, I knew that I needed to give this work a name. It seemed simple. The purpose is college and how to survive the journey: hence, *College Survivor.* My husband had additional suggestions, but I pulled from my own experience as a single parent in college and knew that at that time I was in survival mode. I stood firm with my choice of name.

As time grew closer, I knew that I needed a catchphrase to describe *College Survivor Strategy.* A year later, I sat with my friend J. Sitzmann. While having coffee in our little Iowa town, we played with several phrases, pencil and paper in hand and wheels turning. I must give credit to her support and enthusiasm. With J. Sitzmann's input, we sat together and on a scratch piece of paper, the catchphrase was developed: *Learning the Art and Strategy of Earning Scholarships and Grants from Kindergarten to Graduate School and Beyond.* I knew this phrase captured the core of the book. And so, as that afternoon progressed and after a few emails to my graphic designer at Meta Tech, the catchphrase was added to the front cover.

ABOUT THE AUTHOR

The College Years

In 1989, I graduated with a BA in Speech Communications from Texas A&M University owing $2,300. I was a twenty-three-year-old divorced single parent at that time. I worked. I went to school. I volunteered. I was active in extra-curricular activities, and I raised my toddler son. I had earned several scholarships, including a *Presidential Scholarship*. During my years in college, I had to learn the scholarship, grant, and loan system on my own. I had to learn everything on my own, just like the students today. And just like the students of today, I had to endure the pains of evolving from adolescent to adult. All I could rely on was the mentoring that my parents had provided me while under their wing. My parents were not in a position of assisting financially. I can remember my dad giving me $30. That was the best he could do. But Mom and Dad always brought groceries when they visited me, and they always took care of my son during finals and in the summer. My parents provided moral support and a safe environment for my son when I needed help. If I needed to move, they were all hands on deck. They lived two-and-half hours away and were ready to assist with my son at a moment's notice. This was priceless compared to the $30. Relatives and friends would insult and judge me about pursuing my education and insisted that I should find a local job and raise my child. I would hear things like "you are a bad mother; shame on you," "you are foolish and not thinking straight," "you should put food on the table first and education second." I firmly disagreed, and so did my parents, especially my father. I understood the investment of my time and energy. My son gave me the motivation to push hard. I knew that if I were to live to be seventy or eighty years old, those very short four years (just forty-eight months) of getting an education would provide a life for both of us. I was ready to sacrifice anything and everything to achieve my goals. I knew that the payoff would be huge. And I was right.

Corporate Career

After graduation, doors opened, and I walked right through. I had a wonderful corporate career. I climbed the corporate ladder and won two Presidential Cups. These were the years of my greatest mentoring. I was blessed with amazing leaders that taught me all their secrets to success. Unfortunately, I learned how to become silly rich, and forgot how to be smart poor. Luxury. Pampering. I was a spoiled brat.

Reality Check

Then, all the financial success came to a screeching halt with the birth of our youngest son. At five days old, our youngest son had his first open heart surgery. For nine months, he would turn blue and pass out up to three or four times a week, many times right in my arms. For nine months, he was in and out of the hospital almost every week. At nine months old, he had his second surgery. At three years old, he endured his third surgery. Then, at age ten, he had his fourth surgery with a clear expectation of having additional surgeries every ten years minimum.

Try to imagine the impact on a mother's body… I had numerous medical issues and surgeries of my own from the stress. Stress is destructive. With the loss of our home, we had no choice but to live in a rental house with used cars and depleted funds. We raised the white flag and surrendered to medical bankruptcy. We were no longer silly rich. Now we were forced to be smart poor again and were served humility on a cold plate. That cold plate of humility has kept our family together. We were rich in a different way and wealthier than those with endless finances. I had to use everything I had learned from my college days of how to stretch the dollar so that we could make it. Life lessons are never lost. Blessings of life situations are priceless, especially when you can teach the next generation.

Student Becomes Mentor

In 2016, I was placed in the position of mentor rather than student. Twenty-nine years had passed since my college graduation, and it was time to pass on the torch. We had moved across the country for my husband's job, and I worked as a substitute teacher. This teaching experience was daunting and eye-opening as to what the students of today face and how they make decisions. I had two high school children that were college-bound. I knew our children would be faced with paying for college because of our personal financial situation. I could not believe that I would be placing my own children in the same situation that I was faced with as a college student. Unfathomable. I was determined to teach my children my own methods. I started to research the latest in scholarships and grants. I was prepared for an evolution. I knew I would have to relearn the system. I was wrong. During my research, I found that not much had changed. Just the format. Technology. Parents are still parents. Students are still students. The same questions. The same struggles. Adolescents still develop at the same rate. The one difference that I found was the generation gap and the differences in how parents and students approach higher education because of the generation gap. The research was so intriguing. This is why this subject is approached early in the book.

Back to my research… the internet was chaos. Finding scholarships without knowing how to execute a plan was overwhelming. Then, I decided to order books. The catalog-style books with lists of scholarships were great because I had the scholarships at my fingertips. I read as many first-hand autobiography books as possible, but they were side-tabled because I was not taught how to search, organize and execute a plan. Essentially, all the books or videos would show me *what, where,* and *why.* I could not find a systematic way to execute all the information. I was looking for *how.* I thought, *Someone please help! I have all of this great information, but how do I manage it? How do I organize, execute properly, and do the follow up?* And my biggest question was: *Can you really earn $500,000 in scholarships? Really? Is this realistic?* I felt frustrated again. So I had to devise a system that would work for both of my college-bound children, each facing a road of $130,000 in college costs.

A Research Project. A Workshop. A Book.

I wrote College Survivor (the workbook) by accident. As I researched and researched, hours became days, days became weeks, and weeks became months. I had to begin organizing all of the information in a three-ring binder. Then, I had to add tabs and categories. Before I knew it, I wrote a 150-page workbook. My children's friends began to ask if I could help them, and I did. Then I had a small workshop, and it was amazing. I learned that parents are parents, and students are students, and that nothing has really changed other than technology. And guess what everyone's question was? "How do I organize, execute, and follow up?" Just like me!

The Turning Point

In early fall of 2017, I met two amazing women by happenstance. They both encouraged me to take my original work and publish it as a book. In late fall of 2017, as I talked to personal and business friends about the possibility of publishing a book, I had requests for a Spanish version. I had requests for a chapter devoted to college students. I had requests for a chapter devoted to single parents. The original was designed for high school students. At this point, I knew there was no turning back.

On one very bitter cold day in December 2017, I quit my job, hired my IT guru and in twenty-four hours had a book cover design and logo. In January 2018, with my heart racing, I called a publisher. And here we are…

Next Steps

The greatest request has been to convert this book into a Spanish version. The second request has been to help single parents. These two items are hot on my agenda!

As for me, my dream is to earn my master's and doctorate, debt-free. Trust me, I will not pay a dime! My youngest child has told me that he will earn his doctorate before me! Bring on the challenge, I say. I am a force to be reckoned with.

Final Thoughts

It is my hope that this book will help your family. Every family has unique situations and challenges. Some families have solutions, and some do not. Some families have situations that are traumatic. No matter what, a situation is a moment in time. Tough times don't last; tough people do!

I have spoken with so many parents and students who have fear in their eyes. After a workshop, these parents and students feel as if they have a plan and are filled with hope. Most parents want to see the best for their children and want to support them as best as possible. I have met so many parents and students that just do not know *how*. This is the basis for this book. There are so many amazing resources on the web and in bookstores, and it can be overwhelming to try to develop a plan. I understand being overwhelmed. I remember sitting on my sofa with a plastic bag of information from a college night at my daughter's school and just staring at the wall. I thought to myself, *now what?* That plastic bag sat in the corner of the living room for months and months because I just did not know what to do. One little bag of great information gave me fear. I overcame this fear by developing the *how*. It was no easy task. It included hundreds of hours of research, trial and error, numerous mistakes, and many successes. So, I share my journey and my method with you: *College Survivor Strategy.*

I utilized every ounce of my corporate training, real life experiences, my years as a professional trainer and curriculum writer, and my substitute teacher days to develop this book so that I could convey a plan. My wish is that *College Survivor Strategy* will help your family survive college and help you *learn the art of winning scholarships from kindergarten to graduate school and beyond.*

CREDITS

Photography

Photos with Jazz

Jessica Dawdy, owner

Sioux City, Iowa

https://www.facebook.com/PhotosWithJazz/

Website and Digital Solutions

MetaTech Media

Alex Fuller, founder

Sioux City, Iowa

https://metatechmedia.com/

Publications

Senior Lifestyle Advantage Magazine, Spring 2018

Judith Stanton, Publisher, Editor in Chief

Laurel, Nebraska

https://seniorlifestyleadvantage.com/

Blessed Living News™, Fall 2019

Victor and Diana Morales, Founders, Publishers

Comfort, Texas

http://www.blessedliving-news.com/

Being Better Magazine, Spring 2018

Jennifer Winquist, Founder, Publisher

Sioux City, Iowa

https://www.beingbettermagazine.com/

Financial Advisement, College

Austin Janssen, Janssen Financial Group

North Sioux City, South Dakota

http://www.janssenfinancialgroup.com/

Sources

List of sources available on www.CollegeSurvivorBook.com

Forget
Everything   OR
And
Run

Face
Everything
And
Rise

> *"**Fear** will discourage you from this book. This book will discourage you from **fear.**"*
>
> -P. Solis-Friederich

The **CHOICE** is **YOURS!**